Beside Still Waters

Beside Still Waters

By

Raymond B. Walker, D.D., L.H.D.

Binford & Mort

Thomas Binford, Publisher

2536 S.E. Eleventh • Portland, Oregon 97202

Library of Congress Cataloging in Publication Data

Walker, Raymond B   1888-1974
    Beside still waters.

    1.   Nature (Theology)—Meditations.   I.   Title.
BT695.5.W34   210   75-32601
ISBN 0-8323-0264-3

Foreword

SALUTE TO A CROW

This book began with the raucous caw of a crow.

Daily I had watched the morning sun climb the vine-covered wall and disappear. The window was small, and from the hospital bed all my tired eyes could see was a square of ivy. Plaster contours on the ceiling plagued my fevered imagination and formed fantastic designs. The heat was humid and intense.

I was in revolt against the fate that had canceled interesting summer plans and immobilized me for an indeterminate period. I longed for the sweep of ocean surf, the shaded depths of forest, my suburban garden, dew-drenched at dawn, the familiar bird chorus. But perhaps, even here in the city hospital, I could hear the song of a bird. Long I listened at twilight and dawn, and then one morning, over the muffled roar of the awakening city, it came—not the golden notes of a lark, nor the tentative chirp of a fledgling, but the homely caw of a crow: a song of barnyards, cornfields and wide valleys, sounding over city streets! In that call was a plaintive note as though, lonely in the urban environment, he, too, longed for open spaces and country winds. His repeated caw articulated my mood: it awakened nostalgia and inspired imaginary journeys far from the throngful city ways.

Hour after hour, through the exhausting heat of day and the humid stillness of night, I left that narrow room with its discomforts and austere furnishings to rejoice in the freshness of garden dawn . . . to rest in the cooling peace of evening beside a quiet lake, lulled by the shore-lapping of its ripples . . . I followed trails through mountain canyons where turbulent streams dashed in foaming haste . . . I wandered over damp sand by the sea as the tired tide receded . . . I lay on fragrant clover, watching lazy clouds drift across the sky . . . in breathless wonder I beheld the golden pageantry of dawn and sunset. As I gave myself to such imaginative adventures, there came a miracle of God's out-of-doors; nature's healing peace banished fret, ended revolt, restored serenity! Sleep came again; and soon, my entire being was responding!

Out of that experience came the purpose to collect a group of nature photographs and poems, and to sketch accompanying word-pictures; thus to stimulate imaginative adventures "beside still waters," and help others, denied the out-of-doors, to discover nature paths to serenity and recapture the healing power of God's world of beauty.

All of this the crow's call did for me that morning, as he winged his lumbering way across the city skyline back to his country haunts. His cacophony of raucous discord proved to be joyous music. Not to the meadowlark, the golden-toned thrush, the nightingale of which the poets sing, but to the lowly *Corvus brachyrhynchos* I acknowledge my indebtedness for the inspiration to prepare this book.

Contents

Introduction

THE QUEST FOR SERENITY

Beside Still Waters is intended for lovers of the out-of-doors, especially those who yearn for the quietness and beauty of the open spaces, but are shut-in or duty-bound elsewhere and must, through brief vacation or in memory and imagination, seek rendezvous with nature. The majority of Americans now live in an urban environment. Bumper-to-bumper highway weekend traffic witnesses to an innate hunger for the freedom and tranquility of the out-of-doors.

The chapters of this book have little continuity; open it anywhere and wander through its pages in nostalgic adventure. Linger with the photographs, let them call forth memories of other scenes associated in your experience with serenity and the romance and joy of living. Essays, poems and nature parables are also intended to evoke such memories and to inspire imaginative wanderings in the out-of-doors. Return often to the pictures, not merely to look, but to *feel;* each has its distinctive emotional content; expose yourself unhurriedly to it; brood over it, dream about it, identify yourself with it until you capture the tranquility that it evinces.

How to do it, is the question for which multitudes seek answer: how to relax taut muscles, quiet throbbing nerves, recover calmness and meet with confidence the demands of each new day. This book suggests some simple techniques.

Nature is God's great healer, affording respite from tension and discord. The mysteries and beauties of earth and sea and sky inspire a sense of wonder akin to joy, and instill within the entire being harmony and peace. In your quest for serenity, create a vivid mental picture of some nature refuge; it may be a garden or woodland-bower, a mountain trail or singing stream, a cathedral in the pines with mystical shadows and incense, a cabin in the hills. Such a haven may have been actual in your experience or exist only in imagination, yet even there it can become a reality and your thought-picture a sanctuary where nature's balm heals the spirit. In your day-dreams, visualize it; more importantly, *feel* it; inbreathe its tranquility—your Shangri-La of beauty and joy!

Such use of the imagination is basic in counseling the mentally disturbed. "In the heart lies restlessness or peace"—depending upon the thought processes. Persistently envision defeat and you will *feel* defeated; then you will, in reality, be defeated! By the same process attain victory: visualize yourself achieving; continually dwell upon the implications of success and you will *feel* successful; composed, self-confident, courageous, normal in body functions, vibrant in spirit, serene and joyful. "For as he thinketh in his heart, so is he"[1] declared ancient wisdom. Not analytical is such thinking; rather is it reverie, fantasy, day-dreaming. Picture yourself to yourself as calm, confident, amiable, creative. Hold such a self-image persistently in your thoughts; protect it from negative influence, for as you imagine yourself to be, so you will be! Thinking "in the heart" is simply activating the imagination—the strongest creative force at your disposal. In the quest for serenity, "in quietness and in confidence shall be your strength."[2] The insight of the ancient prophet is confirmed by modern psychotherapy: develop a self-image characterized by serenity and a certainty of achievement, and you will have increasing adequacy in meeting life's demands.

To "rest where you are," substitute for negative moods mental pictures of nature's harmony and peace. Feel the tranquility of hills misty in the distance . . . a spring morning's enchanting fragrance . . . an old road winding through summer woods . . . autumn, in the

country, with its golden torches . . . the harvest moon brilliant over
a quiet valley . . . a friendly lake at sunset, its waves murmuring an
evensong . . . winter's unsullied snowfields reflecting the sun's sparkling smile. As you inbreathe the strength and beauty and joy of
God's creation, into consciousness surges a sense of elation; you are
refreshed and invigorated; nature's healing ministry banishes tension
and fret, restoring harmony in the body. Yes, and spiritual realities
break through the earth's loveliness, as you truly touch the hem of His
garment Whose love shines forth in all His works! Then you will
say, "He leadeth *me* beside the still waters . . . He restoreth *my*
soul!" As your consciousness is thus attuned to Life's Undergirding
Reality, nature will beckon to highways of serenity and joy!

THE CERTAIN CALM

For harassed minds, for hearts assailed by ills,
For all abrasions of the soul, all scars,
There is a panacea of tall hills,
The healing balm of rediscovered stars;
The scent of dew on sleeping ferns and grass,
The flight of homing winds to waiting trees,
And there are clouds that brush the moon and pass . . .
Shadows and dark's pulsating subtleties.
Before the constancy of night and sky,
The certain calm; the peace . . . if any grieves,
He'll shed unhappiness and let it lie
As maples drop their weight of yellow leaves.

Ethel Romig Fuller [3]

MINE

The sun and the moon and the stars are mine,
Rain and the sound of the sea;
The winds that sing in the top of the pine
In wordless harmony.
Ineffable light of the dawn is mine,
Rousing the world from sleep;
Painting the clouds with a color divine.
Grandeur! And mine, to keep!
Mine are the everlasting hills, aflame
With the glory of God;
Flowering fragrance, color and form,
Spring from the lowliest clod.
Mine is the song the stars are singing,
Wheeling across the sky;
Whirling and turning since time's beginning,
Watching the worlds go by.
The night, with its silence and peace is mine,
Marking a rest from strife.
Mine is the earth and the fullness thereof;
Mine is the joy of life!

Peggy James [4]

Beside Still Waters

1

Green Pastures

Blessed are they who can discover a Providence in an enforced relinquishment of activity, and can believe that a Wisdom beyond our own, at times, *maketh* us to "lie down in green pastures" that we may find detachment from consuming busy-ness; freedom from the irritating pressure of too-hurried days, the wear-and-tear of common life; and attain restoration through the healing influence of tranquility. Caught in the maddening haste of our fast-moving world, often we become impervious to life's great essential: a serene mind and a heart filled with patience and love.

The quest for serenity—a flight from reality? The answer depends upon what is meant by reality. If it be beauty, strength, faith in the Eternal Goodness—then to seek such is not flight *from* but *to* reality! Serenity is the primary essential to health of body and spirit.

Pictured here is a quiet meadow—one of nature's sanctuaries. Brood over it; perhaps it quickens the memory of some similar haven from tension known long ago. Visualize that scene of restful beauty; recapture the feeling it inspired.

If your normal life pattern has been interrupted, distorted by weariness or unhappy circumstance, requiring difficult adjustments and perhaps a period of inactivity, accept without rebellion what you cannot now escape, and let the Good Shepherd transform it into a "green pasture" experience! There are compensations even to enforced idleness: hours for meditation denied during normal days; time to read, think, dream, appreciate simple things, renew sensitivity to values obscured during life's feverish routine—also time for visiting lovely islands in the stream of memory.

Now in fancy, recline in the meadow through lazy hours of a summer afternoon, lulled by the earth's gentle breathings: the humming of contented bees. . .the birds' joyous chatter. . .the wind's soft fanning. . .nodding clover, diffusing its fragrance. . .rainbow-hued butterflies happily sailing from blossom to blossom. . .the sun's penetrating warmth. . .shadows dropping upon the field from cumulous clouds as they move slowly across the sky. As you inbreathe nature's calmness, nerves and muscles release their tension; your relaxed mind becomes receptive to Divine Love; you affirm God's unfailing care; tranquility floods your spirit. With quiescence comes imperturbable peace, renewed perspective, and joyous strength! Such serenity will color your thoughts, give vibrancy to your words, and lend grace to your deeds!

As you obey the Shepherd's directive to "lie down in green pastures," you have the joyous consciousness that He will also lead you "beside the still waters," and you gratefully declare, "He restoreth my soul!" In such restoration is fitness for meeting the challenge of life's inevitable shadows with the victorious affirmation, "I will fear no evil!"

Beside Still Waters

THE TWENTY-THIRD PSALM

The Lord is my shepherd;
  I shall not want.
He maketh me to lie down
  in green pastures; He
  leadeth me beside the
  still waters.

He restoreth my soul; He
  leadeth me in the paths
  of righteousness for His
  name's sake.

Yea, though I walk through
  the valley of the shadow
  of death, I will fear no
  evil: for Thou art with
  me; Thy rod and Thy staff
  they comfort me.

Thou preparest a table before
  me in the presence of mine
  enemies: Thou anointest
  my head with oil; my cup
  runneth over.

Surely goodness and mercy
  shall follow me all the
  days of my life: and I
  will dwell in the house
  of the Lord forever.[1]

2

Rejoicing In Beauty

Have you sensitivity to beauty? Can you *feel* as well as see it? Does the loveliness of the world evoke sensation as well as perception? Are you more than vaguely aware of sunset grandeur, bird music, misty horizons? Surrender emotionally to the sublimity of nature; brood over beauty as you come upon it; learn to rejoice in it!

Feel the color ecstasy in the photographs in this book. Attune your spirit to that of its perceptive writers who sing the loveliness of the world. These chapters are vignettes designed to awaken memories, quicken imagination, and inspire delight in seeing, hearing, smelling and feeling nature's wonders.

Love of life involves enjoyment of our Father's world. If, as the Genesis writer declares, "And God saw everything that He had made, and, behold, it was very good,"[1] He must have found infinite satisfaction in creation. God, too, must find joy in His handiwork!

Of the Universality of joy sings the poet:

> All Thy works with joy surround Thee,
> Earth and heaven reflect Thy rays,
> Stars and angels sing around Thee,
> Center of unbroken praise;
> Field and forest, vale and mountain,
> Blossoming meadow, flashing sea,
> Chanting bird and flowing fountain,
> Call us to rejoice in Thee![2]

Beauty is everywhere; cultivate responsiveness to it, sense the joy in it! Envision, now: the iridescence of a soap-bubble floating momentarily in the sunlight. . .a rainbow in the mud, as the puddle is illuminated after the shower. . .the blush on the face of a ripened peach. . .blinking lights of fireflies drifting over a dusk-quiet meadow. Examine a blossom or a snowflake, not with your eyes merely, but with a sense of wonder, as you realize the beauty and intricacies of its formation. Nature is forever luring us to emotional adventure in seeing, listening, touching, loving!

There is ecstasy in the lilting son of a meadowlark. . .exhilaration in the exquisite color-pattern of a butterfly's wings. . .intoxication in the fragrance of rain-washed lilacs. . .delight in the cool caress of morning air. . .tranquility in the enfolding softness of fog . . .solace in the lengthening shadows of eventide. . .restful languor in the weariness that follows the stab of winter's icy breath! All of this is involved in the joy of life. Accept God's world with heightened sensibilities. Cultivate an awareness of His presence—always He is "walking in the garden in the cool of the day!"[3]

Beside Still Waters

> This is my Father's world,
> He shines in all that's fair;
> In the rustling grass I hear Him pass,
> He speaks to me everywhere. [4]

Let beauty get into your consciousness; incorporate it into the very fiber of your being. It will prove to be sustenance for your soul, and essential as is nourishment for your body. Weariness, burden, tension, will vanish; you will be born anew into serenity and freedom of spirit! From adventures in the joy of living, you will turn to common days and tasks refreshed, at peace with life and with the world. One who can retain the capacity for enjoyment of God's world of beauty has the secret of abiding youth: buoyancy, creativity, a vibrant and happy spirit!

FOR THE BEAUTY OF THE EARTH

> For the joy of ear and eye,
> For the heart and mind's delight,
> For the mystic harmony
> Linking sense to sound and sight;
> Lord of all, to Thee we raise
> This, our hymn of grateful praise.

Folliott S. Pierpoint [5]

3

To Love A Garden

To love a garden is to *feel* as well as see its
enchanting beauty, to sense its mystical quality
as did the poet of old, who declared that God
walked there in the cool of the day. Put, now,
your mood in step with Him and wander paths of
loveliness in some memory bower or in the
garden of your dreams.

Feel joyously the garden's beauty: ordered
serenity of hedge and tree and plant, reaches
of carpet-green merging into a riot of variegated
blossoms; here is a color symphony as stirring to
the soul as that of music: minor notes are the
shadows. . .in thin tones sunlight filters through
leafy boughs. . .with soft whispers blade and bloom
respond to wind-fingers' light caress.

Lingering in memory are nostalgic garden odors,
nature's incense evoking a mood—haunting and

intangible, a reach for something which words can
never express; feel again the scent of blossom
fragrance. . .the earth's warm dampness. . .acrid pungence ·
of dried stalks. . .the sweet drift of newly cut grass. . .
        the freshness of a lily pool.

To love a garden is to recapture its tranquility:
butterflies twinkle, bees drone their work song,
hummingbirds hover at honey-laden blooms; and as
the shadows lengthen and the winds sleep, beauty broods
        and peace banishes care and fret.

From far years your garden memories may come—
a loveliness more emotional than visual, and that
transforms restlessness to repose. But if yours
is a dream garden, a figment of your imagination,
it, too, may minister nature's calm, and bestow
        a benediction of peace.

For, still, in the cool of the day, perceptive
souls are aware of the Unseen Presence amid the
garden beauty; and serenity, gift of Divine Love,
        heals the hurts of life.

MY GARDEN

A garden is a lovesome thing, God wot!
Rose plot,
   Fringed pool,
Fern's grot—
   The veriest school
   Of peace; and yet the fool
Contends that God is not—
Not God! in gardens! When the eve is cool?
   Nay, but I have a sign;
   'Tis very sure God walks in mine.

Thomas Edward Brown [1]

4

Moment Of Splendor

Sunset is the Infinite Artist's masterpiece; its beauty not only to be seen but felt. And yet, numberless sunsets are wasted upon unfeeling observers—moments of splendor to which the spirit is impervious; not that one is incapable of sensitivity but because the faculty has been neglected, and the usual, even though it be the beautiful, is relegated to the prosaic and commonplace. One may be aware of beauty and yet not experience it.

If only once in a century, the sun, robed in majestic splendor, passed from sight, what world-wide commotion would attend the event! What anticipations and memories would be provoked; long would the phenomenon be discussed and the last living witness sought for reminiscence! Perhaps out yonder in the immensities of space are planets so huge that their sunsets occur but once in a life-span such as ours. If perceptive beings are there, imagine what a sunset must mean!

Here on our small earth, nature's pageants of beauty are constantly recurring: sunsets in spring, summer, autumn, winter—no two

29

alike, each with its distinctive coruscations of splendor, as the day wrapped in golden garments joins yesterday in the annals of time.

For the connoisseur of esthetics, sunsets are among life's richest joys: heart-lifting strains in God's symphony of visual sublimity—on prairie's far horizon. . .beyond glistening mountain peaks. . . through leafy bowers of forestry. . .at sea amid trailing brilliance. . . on the skyline of man's habitations where spires reach upward against a backdrop of lambent flame. For those who love beauty and have eyes to see and hearts to feel, truly, "the heavens declare the glory of God!"[1]

It is said that the complete brilliance of a sunset lasts but seconds; it crescendos to its color apex and immediately begins to decline. The artist breathlessly awaits the climax—the moment of splendor with its ecstatic beauty and joyous wonder.

There are moments of splendor in human experience, when the ineffable glory of being breaks over the soul: exalted glimpses of life's meaning and purpose, mystic visions of that Reality which we call God—a spiritual glow comparable to a glorious sunset. Too profound for words is such a baptism of beauty; it cannot be described, it can only be felt. In such a moment of splendor we sense the rhythm and joy and wonder of life, although we cannot articulate it. Perhaps it was in such a mood that Milton said, "What if earth be but the shadow of heaven!" Ever the sensitive soul reaches toward the ultimate, the ineffable! Such is our destiny! Truly did Francis Thompson sing:

> O world invisible, we view thee,
>   O world intangible, we touch thee,
> O world unknowable, we know thee,
>   Inapprehensible, we clutch thee![2]

Beside Still Waters

Brood over this summer sunset photograph: let its moment of splendor symbolize the quest of your spirit and bring joy to your heart!

THE WORLD

O Earth! thou hast not any wind that blows
Which is not music; every weed of thine
Pressed rightly flows in aromatic wine;
And every humble hedgerow flower that grows,
And every little brown bird that doth sing,
Hath something greater than itself, and bears
A living Word to every living thing,
Albeit it holds the Message unawares.
All shapes and sounds have something that is not
Of them: a Spirit broods amid the grass;
Vague outlines of the Everlasting Thought
Lie in the melting shadows as they pass;
The touch of an Eternal Presence thrills
The fringes of the sunsets and the hills.

Richard Realf [3]

GOD IS AT THE ANVIL

God is at the anvil, beating out the sun;
  Where the molten metal spills,
At His forge among the hills
  He has hammered out the glory of a
    day that's done.

God is at the anvil, welding golden bars;
  In the scarlet-streaming flame
He is fashioning a frame
  For the shimmering silver beauty of
    The evening stars.

Lew Sarett [4]

5

Rainbow After The Shower

Nothing in nature evokes such delight or gives a greater lift to the spirit than the rainbow. It is a witness of triumph, the prophecy of smiling skies. Clouds may yet darken but the storm's fury is spent; the morrow will be fair! Ever the eye follows, and likewise the heart, the dipping arch to where its multi-colored splendor meets the earth and kisses ordinary things with radiance, revealing amid the commonplace the dreamed-of pot of gold.

The rainbow's lilting beauty is possible only because the sky has been darkened by storm clouds. Thus hope shines across life's falling tears and enables the sufferer to reveal against the background of dark hours the radiance of faith, lifting the spirits of those who behold. Courage amid tragedy, patience through suffering, hope despite weariness, faith in Divine Goodness even when evil overshadows—these form one of life's most inspiring creations: the rainbow of an undefeated soul!

As every raindrop is a prism through which white light rays are broken into colors of arching beauty, so human tears may become prisms of faith—transmuting sorrow, loneliness, disappointment and pain into creative loveliness.

Storms may buffet your life, clouds hang dark and heavy, yet you may reflect immortal beauty, your days iridescent with God's love, creating a rainbow to bless, inspire and give joy to others!

33

6

Waters That Laugh And Sing

Little rivers and rollicking mountain streams smile
as they silver the landscape. They also sing.
    Happy in their wanderings,
with laughter they leap in white foam over great rocks,
and ripple with glee crossing beds of little pebbles.
They glide into tranquil pools beneath sheltering branches,
only to hurry out again in the indomitable haste ever
    characteristic of flowing waters.

Always, in active water there is music: the soft cooing
tones of infancy as the streamlet trickles from melting
snowbank or quietly bubbling spring. . .liquid notes of
idleness as though, repenting of haste, the brook
    hesitates in its course. . .
murmurs of contentment as the stream glides through
grassy banks. . .happy gurglings of eager waters dancing
into rapids. . .the strong voice of maturity when the
    river becomes a sonorous torrent.
Tones vary from the limpid whisper of a tiny brook to the
    bold thunder of the mighty cascade.

Of what do they sing, these moving waters? Their theme
is purpose: they know and seek their destiny. In the
song are refrains of happy adventure: they have known
    mountain splendor and meadow stillness. . .

have been kissed by amber dawns and caressed by silver
moonbeams. . .replenished from bursting clouds and
    purified by precipice plunge. . .
in moments of calmness they have mirrored sunset skies.
    Not content with these,
they sing of joys they yet shall know. Every bend lures,
every horizon beckons to the last and most beautiful of
all adventures when, in ecstasy, they fling themselves into
    the timeless embrace of Mother Sea!

Not without opposition the stream achieves its destiny:
when it cannot rise above a frowning blockade, the waters
channel a course around it and with triumphant chuckles
    hurry onward.

For us also life has been endowed with purpose and problems.
Waters that laugh and sing bid us meet obstacles with bold
and joyous maneuvers, bypassing the inevitable. Jesus'
exhortation, "Say unto this mountain, remove hence to
yonder place,"[1] dramatizes the stratagem of faith.
    Massive obstruction may appear,
yet for the undaunted soul there is a way onward. Detours
there may need be, but no deadends. Then laugh and sing,
for the way leads onward and upward, and forever
    the best is yet to be!

"God saw everything that He had made and. . .it was very
good."[2] Surely it was with rapture that He beheld
    His creation so vibrant with energy and joy.
Shall not man made in His image share this elemental
gladness? Declared the ancient prophet, "The Lord thy
God will rejoice over thee with joy. . .He will joy over
thee with singing."[3] Then let our lives be joyous
and beautiful, as our Creator intends them ever to be:
    full of laughter and song!

Beside Still Waters

FROM "THE BROOK"

I chatter over stony ways,
   In little sharps and trebles,
I bubble into eddying bays,
   I babble on the pebbles.
With many a curve my banks I fret
   By many a field and fallow,
And many a fairy foreland set
   With willow-weed and mallow.
I chatter, chatter, as I flow
   To join the brimming river;
For men may come and men may go,
   But I go on forever.
I wind about, and in and out,
   With here a blossom sailing,
And here and there a lusty trout,
   And here and there a grayling,
And here and there a foamy flake
   Upon me, as I travel
With many a silvery waterbreak
   Above the golden gravel.
I slip, I slide, I gloom, I glance,
   Among my skimming swallows,
I make the netted sunbeam dance
   Against my sandy shallows.
I murmur under moon and stars
   In brambly wildernesses;
I linger by my shingly bars;
   I loiter round my cresses;
And out again I curve and flow
   To join the brimming river,
For men may come and men may go,
   But I go on forever.

Alfred Tennyson

7

The Silences Of God

Who—sleepless, troubled, sorrowing—has not in the quiet night gazed with wonder into the glowing heavens! Through uncounted ages, the stars have given comfort to restless human hearts; their beauty and constancy have, in eloquent silence, bestowed a benediction of peace.

Encircled we are by planets and galaxies, in number baffling both mathematics and imagination, more numerous than all the grains of sand on all the seashores of our earth, enough for every human being from the beginning of time to have had a world all his own, with uncountable billions left over for present and future generations! Silently, these planets in their appointed orbits wheel through space. In the luminous splash that we call the Milky Way, our earth—tiny in comparison with many of its neighbors—speeds on its course a thousand miles a minute; but have you ever felt the slightest vibration from its movement? It swings on its axis twenty-five thousand miles every twenty-four hours, yet without confusion or clamor! Brightly the constellations smile down upon us, testifying to the silences of the Creator—a Wisdom infinite in power, timeless in purpose, Whose grandeur the serene heavens declare!

39

"Study to be quiet," admonished the Apostle Paul to harassed souls of his simple, agrarian age. Today, the clamorous dissonance of noises created by the machinery of modern civilization beats upon us with tragic insistence, threatening health of body and peace of mind. Yet, escape there is for those who have learned the healing solitudes of nature: the hush of a deep forest. . .the hush of a mountain canyon. . .the almost inaudible murmur of a wandering brook . . .the sunset's panorama of muted color. . .the silent splendor of the star-studded sky.

The real purpose of fishing, according to Isaac Walton, consists not in the catch but the haunting seclusion into which the sportsman's quest has lured him: the brooding calm of nature bringing peace to his soul. So—if not in actuality, then in memory or in imagination—go often to some such sanctuary where clamor would seem a sacrilege and "study to be quiet."

It is the impact of vibrations upon consciousness that produces noise. Tumultuous and incessant may be such bombardment in the world of matter, yet it is possible to tune out the distracting din and know the harmonies of an order in which the material is but a tiny island in a measureless ocean of reality: a super-realm—vast, unsearchable, invisible, ultimate and abiding—the domain of spirit. That is our native land! There we belong! It is an area that the din and hurry of days cannot invade, for we are essentially spirit. And, "God is spirit," declared Jesus. We are made in the likeness of our Creator! The ancient directive, "Be still and know that I am God,"[1] is meaningful today. In the midst of the blatant dissonance of our world, one can maintain communion with the Eternal Reality and experience what the older mystics termed "peace at the center." Amid feverish pressures, distracting noises, a discordant or even hostile environment, one may within himself possess a secret sanctuary, there to "be still and know" the healing joy of creative serenity.

Beside Still Waters

Seek the soothing ministry of God's silences! Let His peace flow into your consciousness as light streams through the portals of dawn . . .as the wind drifts fresh and clean across spring-kissed hills. . .as the sea floods creeks and inlets with its renewing tide. . .as the velvet hangings of night noiselessly unveil the smiling stars! Let stillness enter your being; inbreath it; feel it; know it—the calm of the universe, the healing hush of the Infinite, the brooding presence of Divine Love! "Be still and know," and you will (in the words of Max Ehrmann) "go placidly amid the noise and the haste, and remember what peace there may be in silence!"

I HAVE KNOWN A SOUND

I have known a sound so full of music
It echoes through the high peaks of my mind:
The clear, cold sound of running mountain water
Taking its swift way seaward, there to find
A deeper music in the ocean's vastness;
But, oh, the lovely solo that it plays
Moving across wet rocks down spruce-dark canyons,
Flute to its lips and piping its sweet lays.

Often I hear it over miles of distance,
Often it sounds across wide leagues of air:
The rippling music, the high silver fluting
Of water stepping among wet stones, somewhere,
And on the high peaks of my mind are echoes
Clear and sweet as the flute notes strike them there.

Grace Noll Crowell[2]

8

Seaside Healing

THE FACE OF THE SEA—
A-shimmer with silver, as the sun
    lavishes radiance upon it. . .
A-gleam with gold, as the flaming orb
    dips into the horizon. . .
Blue, as the benign heavens smile. . .
White-flecked, as hastening winds
    whip across its waters. . .
Leaden, as dull clouds gray the sky. . .
Somber in darkening anger, as the
    storm beats against it. . .
Smiling, as beneath a brilliant moon
    every wave-crest catches a
    fleeting sparkle of copper. . .
The mercurial Sea—quick to change its
    countenance and reflect nature's
    every passing mood!

THE GROPING FINGERS OF THE SEA—

The ceaseless drama of the tide:
Ever moving toward that mysterious
        moment when its cycle is renewed;
Leaving upon receptive sands the marks
        of its coming and going:
Strange hieroglyphics, written as by
        the finger of Infinity!
When the tide's cleansing cycle is complete,
Debris has been swept away. . .
Sands laundered—washed and ironed. . .
        marks of beach traffic removed. . .
        furrows and ridges all smoothed again.
Adorned, now, with jewels are the Sea's
        shoulders—glittering stones,
        scalloped shells, ocean flowers:
Mysterious gifts from another shore!

THE VOICE OF THE SEA—

From the distance an undistinguishable
        roar of sound, melting to a whisper
        as one recedes. . .nearer, the
        monotone punctuated by occasional
        rushes of noise, as wild breakers crash. . .
Momentary cessations there are, as though
        the Ocean were holding its breath.
There is music in the mighty cadences,
        murmuring whispers, and silences of
        the rhapsodical Sea!

Beside Still Waters

IF YOU KNOW AND LOVE THE SEA—

Wander, now, in fancy along its shore. . .
    spirit attuned to its beauty. . .
    heart rested by its music. . .
    fret swept away in its renewing tide. . .
    soul refreshed by its energizing wind!
Inbreathe the healing power of the Sea,
    and receive God's gift of peace!
Salute in joy its mystic horizon: symbol of
    the soul's quest that gives
    life meaning and purpose and infinity!

FAR BEYOND

We can only see a little of the ocean,
    Just a few miles distant from the rocky shore;
But out there—far beyond our eyes' horizon,
    There's more—immeasurably more.

We can only see a little of God's loving—
    A few rich treasures from His mighty store;
But out there—far beyond our eyes' horizon,
    There's more—immeasurably more. [1]

9

God's Mirror

Only still waters can reflect nature's splendor.

Serenity is not attained by exertion—only in quietness
of soul is it realized, for tranquility and peace are
reflected virtues.

How shall you learn to be still?
Leave the disturbing moment where gusts of pain or
drifts of weariness ruffle your spirit; go in memory or
imagination to nature's still waters: some quiet pool
where majesty is mirrored. Turbulence would erase the
beauty and distort the reflection of surrounding
loveliness. Sang the Psalmist: "He leadeth me beside
still waters". . .let the Shepherd of Serenity guide
your thoughts, your mood and you will attain the calmness
that banishes distortion.

All about you are the glories of life: the beauty and
strength of the universe, the changeless love of God.

47

These are the eternal realities. Fret is but the wind
that riffles, pain the storm that disrupts, fear the
turbulence that destroys. Freedom from such agitation?
As of old, One speaks: "Peace, be still," [1]
rebuking all that disturbs the soul's tranquility.

God is the Creator and man is intended to be His image
and likeness. Let Divine Perfection, the Eternal Reality,
dominate and you will reflect only loveliness and peace,
for you are God's mirror!

OUT IN THE FIELDS WITH GOD

The little cares that fretted me
   I lost them yesterday,
Among the fields above the sea,
   Among the winds at play,
Among the lowing of the herds,
   The rustling of the trees,
Among the singing of the birds,
   The humming of the bees.

The foolish fears of what might happen,
   I cast them all away
Among the clover-scented grass,
   Among the new-mown hay,
Among the husking of the corn,
   Where drowsy poppies nod,
Where ill thoughts die and good are born—
   Out in the fields with God.

Elizabeth Barrett Browning [1]

Beside Still Waters

IN A QUIET VALLEY

Here I have found a respite from my sorrow,
Here I have found a solace for my grief,
And yesterday, today, and each tomorrow
Are lightened by this exquisite relief.

I shall rest here awhile, I shall be staying,
Steeping my soul in solitude and peace;
Over and over again, I shall be saying
One prayer, until the quivering hurt shall cease.

Here God has cupped His gracious hand to hold me.
Here are His winds, the grass, the arching sky,
Here is the kindly Mother-earth to mold me
Into her own calm image as I lie.

You who have known but city street and alley,
You who are weary, waiting for grief to cease,
Seek through the world until you find this valley,
It has the strength and power to bring you peace.

Grace Noll Crowell [2]

10

Our Daily Bread

*A*rcheological discoveries reveal wheat as the oldest of all cultivated plants, ancient as civilization itself. It is a fragile crop, threatened by many enemies: insects, disease, weeds, wind and hail. Modern science cannot protect it from the elements, but much has been done to combat other hazards. Breathlessly, the hungry markets of the world await its harvest!

Across America's immense "bread basket" stretch fields of golden grain. Thousands of towering elevators punctuate horizons: storage for nature's beauty, ere—by various journeys and processes—it becomes loaves in the homes of our own and other lands.

Wheat is among the most beautiful of productive grasses. Unforgettable is the sight of ripened grain undulating in the summer wind, its golden billows surging into prairie distance. Friendly zephyrs have moved across the fields, caressing the stigmas, and at nature's chosen moment, blessing them with pollen; also causing every spike, minute flower, featherly finger and ripening head to vibrate—thus sounding forth music; and now in maturity, all join in the golden dance and rippling song of the wheat.

51

No delicate perfume, no pungent odor does it possess until it reaches the oven. Is there a more delightful and mouth-watering fragrance than that of baking bread?

In the rippling fields of gold, nature's chemical miracle transmutes sunlight into substance wherewith our physical bodies are nourished. Sunlight is the origin and source of all energy for hearty, healthy, happy living. The alchemy through which comes our daily bread is saturated with wonder and beauty.

> Back of the loaf is the snowy flour,
>   And back of the flour the mill;
> And back of the mill is the wheat, and
>   the shower,
>   And the sun, and the Father's will.[1]

Animating the creative process: life and its sustenance—is Divine Purpose, a scheme of Infinite Love, "The Father's will." See and feel it in the pulsating beauty of the billowing grain, golden in warm vitality—blessed by the sunlight! The One Who taught us to pray, "Give us this day our daily bread," also declared, "Man shall not live by bread alone." There are hungers other than physical. Through faith, hope and love, sustenance is generated for the spirit. By beauty, also, the inner self is nourished and enriched.

Our daily bread is served to us on golden platters. In splendor comes the harvest: fields of ripened grain. . .trees laden with sun-kissed fruit. . .vines heavy with clusters of purple grapes.

All the gifts of Nature are rendered to us in beauty. No drab, somber, colorless creation sustains us; its munificence includes a bonus of loveliness! Splendor there is everywhere for those who have eyes to see and hearts to feel; truly asks the poet, "God, how can you think of such lovely things, such beauty for night and day?"[2]

Beside Still Waters

Counseled Charles Kingsley, "Never lose an opportunity to see anything beautiful, for beauty is God's handwriting." More than His handwriting, it is His loving smile; indeed, it is an attribute of Himself. Thus it becomes part of our daily bread, not a luxury but a necessity. With it the soul is fed! Give thanks unto God for beauty!

Surrender to the influence of beauty: the gift of Divine Love! Let the promise be fulfilled: "That your joy may be full."[3] In that abundance you will join "the song of the wheat," of the shower and the sun, indeed, the song of all creation, rejoicing in the Father's will!

BREAD

Wheat is still. It makes no sound
As it pushes from the ground.

As it runs its slow, serene
Course in rows of tender green.

Wheat is quiet; as it grows
It only whispers what it knows.

Wheat is mute—till it is fed
To children as a loaf of bread.

Then it is laughter; it is song;
It is clamor all day long.

Ethel Romig Fuller [4]

11

Beyond The Horizon

Purple mountains against a cloud-furrowed sky—an enchanting horizon that lures the spirit past shadowed recesses and jagged summits, inspiring eagerness to explore regions beyond!

So it is with horizons: the long line at sea where in mystic haze ocean lifts to merge with sky. . .far-flung reaches of prairie with an infinitude of blue dipping down to caress earth's edge. . .mountain ranges mantled with glistening snow. . .distant masses of trees dim in shadowed tracery. . .a church spire rising above city roofs, faith's punctuation mark on the skyline.

Horizons stir the heart to inarticulate longing for the unknown, the beyond, that which lies past the mysterious edge—the boundary of the visible.

No horizon is a finality. When you reach yonder place where sky and earth seem now to meet, you find them as far apart there as here. In truth, you can't reach the horizon; it isn't there; it exists only in your eyes and mind! As long as life moves forward, it leads to new vistas beyond. The horizon is, indeed, "God's signature against the sky." His assurance of on-going life, His challenge to the Adventure Splendid! "There's no end, jes' goin' on and on,"[1] as the beloved song declares!

Every tomorrow is another horizon. Let your heart be glad! Let your spirit sing! Even that "last frontier," of which we sadly speak, is only an illusion, a figment of mortal understanding. When we approach it, that frontier, also, will vanish and before us will stretch vistas of infinity—the life eternal! To the adventure of being, there is no end. The pledge? God's signature written in mystic beauty against our sky!

12

Vistas Of Peace

Mountains and seas are the most spectacular phases of creation —the most sought and loved by man. When the Psalmist cried, "I will lift up mine eyes unto the mountains,"[1] he expressed a universal human aspiration.

Mountain ranges, and especially the peaks, have their own individuality. Each is unlike any other. Among the best known and loved are the towering Alps with Jungfrau and the Matterhorn, the gentle Appalachians with Mount Washington, the rugged Rockies with McKinley and Pike, the mighty Cascades with Rainier, Hood and Shasta, the jagged Sierras with Mount Whitney; each different in beauty, form, and challenge.

But, all mountains are whimsical, ofttimes hiding from valley-dwellers who in vain lift up their eyes. Yet, when least expected, they appear again in shining glory, as wondrous jewels set upon the horizon. Some days, with not a cloud in the heavens, the mountains stand stark against the infinite blue. From the chill splendor of sunrise, until the warm rose of evening afterglow, is unrolled the panorama of majestic beauty. Unforgettable the picture: green valley, purple-shadowed hills, wrinkled reaches of forestry, and finally the summit's eternal snows gleaming in the sky, bathed in exquisite shades of shifting color.

What is the secret of the mountains' lure? Breath-taking beauty, yes, but also mystic silence. How different from the sea, which is never silent: it roars anger, shouts challenge, sobs loneliness, croons peace. But soundless are the mighty peaks. It was not always so. In tumultuous violence were the mountains' beginnings: molten convulsions, eons of hardening crusts, millenniums of grinding ice, ages of jagged chaos, but at last silence, tranquility—and vistas of peace!

Naturalist John Muir, with heightened sensibilities, studied and explored mountains and left this admonition: "Climb the mountains and get their good tidings. Nature's peace will flow into you as sunshine flows into the trees. The winds will blow their own freshness into you and the storms their energy, while cares will drop off like autumn leaves."[2]

In the presence of towering grandeur the Psalmist asked, "From whence cometh my help?" The silent guardians proclaimed a Source of strength beyond his own. The mountains' tranquility so permeated his consciousness that he could close his eyes and yet see the symbol of his reinforcement—a mystic Reality by which to orient his life, even through days of clouded vision. We, also, with unfaltering certitude, may know the Strength from which our help cometh, even though about us the fogs are dense! And out of the tumult of days we may emerge to abiding peace!

To valley-dwellers, mountain influence is inculcated into the very texture of common life. Obscured by clouds, neglected amid the pressure of affairs, yet the ranges remain a dominant force; climate, agriculture and commerce depend upon them. In their reservoirs are vast supplies of water; in their plunging torrents, energy for light, warmth and industry. And so we are sure of the mountains, not because with ecstasy we, on occasion, gaze upon their beauty or recapture in memory or photograph their soul-lifting splendor. Dependable and dominant they are to our very existence.

Muir bade us "climb the mountains and get their good tidings." Ever they symbolize the Heights from which cometh our strength and with the Psalmist we joyfully declare, "My help cometh from the Lord Which made heaven and earth!"

Lift your eyes to Vistas of Peace and hear the mountains' soundless voice speak of God!

WHO KNOWS A MOUNTAIN?

Who knows a mountain?
  One who has gone
To worship its beauty
  In the dawn;
One who has slept
  On its breast at night;
One who has measured
  His strength to its height;

One who has followed
  Its longest trail,
And laughed in the face
  Of its fiercest gale;
One who has scaled its peaks,
  And has trod
Its cloud-swept summits
  Alone with God.

Ethel Romig Fuller [3]

13

The House And The Road

There's something about a quiet road winding into the distance that sets the heart dreaming. As the road disappears around the bend or drops from sight over the hill, it leaves behind the haunting lure of the unexplored farness. The unknown beckons! There is, oft-times, exhilaration in the mere thought of going somewhere. Misty horizons. . .singing streams. . .flaming colors of springtime-bloom or autumn-blaze. . .radiant mountain summits against an amethyst sky. . .winter stillness with inky etchings of tree shadows across the clean snow: the enchanting beyond—golden miles unveiling new beauty, promising new interests and tasks, new friends and joys, life more thrilling in its abundance!

And, there's something about a quiet house at the foot of a wooded hill where the road goes by, that tugs at the heartstrings: cheery hearth-fire. . .cozy comforts. . .potted geraniums in the windows. . .rooms redundant with memories. . .lilac bushes with purple spears guarding the gate! The little House symbolizes serenity and seems to contradict the call of the Road.

Which is right, Road or House? *Go* or *Stay*? Both are right! The duality that they represent is essential for wholesome, normal living.

Every individual needs stability but also stimulus, alternation between security and adventure that life may be kept fresh, joyous and creative!

Mere security easily begets passivity; life that has reached a dead-level faces deterioration; unused powers atrophy. Normalcy demands the rhythm of rest and activity, the going-in to quiet composure and the going-out to action. The mind that settles into a groove of unstirred routine suffers boredom; monotony is debilitating; emotions that are curbed by fixations become shallow and stagnant. Yes, we need the Road's challenge to move on.

Change that interrupts established patterns is often regarded as one of life's cruelties; actually, it may be a benefactor; all depends upon how we meet it, what we do with it. When change stimulates alertness, awakens fresh interests, requires new adjustments, it transforms life into a glorious quest and inspires us to meet it with eagerness!

But, however thrilling our work and challenging our interests, there must be periods for rest, recuperation, the inflow of energy. Betimes we must heed the invitation of the little House to linger, which means to pause and seek the healing ministry of quietude, that the fret of tensions may be banished, and the spirit renewed in courage and strength. Tranquility is not an end in itself, for such is negative. Effective relaxation opens channels for fresh energy; creative serenity becomes a joyous dynamic—a purpose to know more, be more, do more. The positive life is a glorious venture in making one's days meaningful.

What if, because of duty elsewhere, you cannot actually escape to what the little House symbolizes? Then, in memory, return to dear, familiar places: scenes of beauty and peace, recapturing something of the serenity of former days. Or, in imagination, inspired by pictures of outdoor loveliness, visualize yourself absorbing nature's tranquillity, and so find healing release from strain and fatigue.

What if, because of infirmity or other confining circumstance, you cannot leave your little House for adventures of the Road? You can travel afar even though you must remain at home! You can stay and also go! In that paradox is one of life's dearest truths. Where one lives is not so much a matter of geography as interests. The size of your world, its beauty and its adventurous qualities depend upon your powers of perception and imagination. Confined to your little House you may yet know nature's beauty and the wonders of God's great out-of-doors.

Passing your open door is the human procession—voices echoing to your heart the problems and hopes of mankind. Marching by are causes and crusades challenging your participation with knowledge and enthusiasm—and, always, the undergirding influence of prayer. From your little House you can project yourself into other lives, inspiring accomplishments which for you personally are impossible. Thus, you may help to change the world—Keep the door open wide!

The adventures of the Road—the security of the House; life is not complete until it includes both! God is not only our Inspiration to all worthy undertakings; He is also our "Dwelling Place"; He is both life's supreme quest and its ultimate stability: "God is our refuge and strength."[1] In the rhythm between stimulus and security is the divine law of growth and joy. Long ago the Psalmist declared it: "The Lord shall preserve thy *going out* and thy *coming in* from this time forth, and even forevermore."[2]

14

Ships Of Rest

Do you remember the clouds of childhood?
Go back across the years: lie on the meadow's
    thick grass, watching the fantastic
    shape of cloud formations.
Feel the warm restfulness of the summer sun
    darkened by intermittent shadows. . .
Smell the clover fragrance in the drifting
    breeze. . .
Hear the drowsy song of contentment as bees
    wing from blossom to blossom.
Across the sky float faces, animals, ships
    and castles. . .
A panorama of soft clouds, their pattern
changing with each leisurely movement.

Let these soothing memories induce rest.
Even as childhood's ships of fancy wafted
    you to dreamland,
now follow the fleecy harbingers of peace
until, with delicious languor, drowsiness
creeps upon you; the world of sense fades
away and the old promise is fulfilled:
"Thou shall lie down, and thy sleep shall
    be sweet." [1]

Perhaps you wondered whether those fleecy masses
    might be the ermine robes of God.
Well, God is in His sky today no less than
in those hours of childhood faith and fantasy.
His snowy argosies are sailing through the
seas of space laden with rest for you.
Inbreathe His peace: let tense nerves
relax, tired muscles sag, your mind
drift as you follow God's ships of rest.
To your receptive spirit they bear cargoes
    of serenity!

WORDS OF GOD

Every bird that sings
And every flower that stirs the elastic sod,
And every breath the fragrant summer brings
To the pure spirit is a Word of God.

Samuel Taylor Coleridge [2]

Beside Still Waters

HOW LOVELY IS THE HAND OF GOD

I sometimes think when silvery light
Floods land and sea with moonbeams bright,
How lovely is the hand of God
That smooths the rough road man has trod,
How wonderful His love must be
To give the moon, the land, the sea!

How lovely is the hand of God,
That heals with flowers the broken rod,
Takes up the thing man spoils in vain
To mould and make it fair again.
O Love, so wide, so deep, so free,
Let me forever be lost in Thee! [3]

15

Valley Of Peace

*L*ate summer. . .the heat lingers. . .

The dew-washed breath of the morning is fresh with clover-sweetness. . .serenity broods over the valley, its silence broken by the slow tone of cowbells, the hum of insects, the twitter of birds, the joyous bark of a dog from a distant farmstead. The feeling of Sabbath is in the air. . .man has ceased from toil to praise his Creator; the church-bell's mellow tones drift over hill and dale.

From a grove near the chapel bursts a bird-anthem, while on a near fencepost a meadowlark sings and the hum of bees softly caresses the quiet air, like the whisper-tones of an organ.

Feel the poignant tranquility of this scene! Here are simple things touched with beauty. Let the peace of God enter your spirit with healing power as you brood over the picture: woodpile, wire-fence, weather-beaten barn in contrast with the neatly painted church. . .all kissed by the early sun casting long shadows over the hillsides. . . here common things glow with uncommon beauty. Return in memory to *your* Valley of Peace. . .contentment is there, amid the old and familiar. . .such as is not to be found in the new and the strange.

Recapture God's gift of serenity. . .let your spirit be at peace!

16

Liquid Poem

A stream suddenly becomes a poem!
Plunging over the rocky ledge,
its waters drop with lilting grace:
sparkling with beauty, white, lacy—
an ethereal veil flung against the
    shoulder of the hill.

A once prosaic brook now becomes a
backdrop for rainbows: broken to bits,
its shattered fragments merge into the
breath-taking loveliness of the falls.
No more perfect grace exists in nature,
unless it be the delicate tracery of
maidenhair fern, guarded by damp trees
and caressed by the fall's hovering mist.

Feel its moist breath upon your face—
drifting in the breeze, a brooklet's kiss.
The sweet shock of its cool touch quiets
    life's fever, induces God's peace.

Let the Beauty that merges the broken
fragments of a stream into a plunge of
splendor, gather your weariness and pain
into something unutterably lovely!
Against falling tears gleam rainbows of
    the soul's triumph!

Let your faith in Eternal Beauty, like
the liquid poem, drift out to quiet and
inspire others. Thus your prosaic and
even tragic days may become one of God's
    blessed poems of grace!

17

The Trees Of Home

Who, in times of anxiety and weariness—or enforced interruption of normal life activity—has not, in memory, returned to childhood scenes and moods, seeking surcease in the carefree gaiety, simple faith and tranquility of youth?

> The hills are dearest, which our childish feet
> Have climbed the earliest; and the streams
>   most sweet
> Are ever those at which our young lips drank,
> Stooped to their water o'er the grassy bank.[1]

There were also scarlet sumac, plumes of goldenrod, brown-eyed susans, field daisies and elusive violets. In leafy hiding places were wild strawberries, warm and plump and juicy.

And who can forget the trees of home—majestic and friendly, reaching forth strong limbs for shelter, also as an invitation to adventurous climbing! In springtime the birds built nests in the high branches, sang their joy and taught their young the arts of winged life.

73

Among the trees were maples—in the spring with bursting buds, in autumn gaily clad in red and yellow. . .elms, stately and austere. . . birch, straight and white, upon whose stripped bark were penned childish notes. . .massive oaks with clinging leaves sighing wearily through winter storms, and sadly drifting away when spring buds demanded their lodgments. . .and other trees there were, loved for their gifts of fruit and nuts.

Hanging from strong limbs were rope swings, in which one could "pump" to thrilling heights; hammocks for the less daring were suspended between willing trunks; and as high as possible from the ground were tree-houses—some mere platforms laboriously built by young hands, others roofed and sided with the help of indulgent grown-ups.

The tree-house was a childhood sanctuary: an escape from the adult world, affording secrecy for day-dreaming, the sharing of confidences with playmates, discussion of the strange ways of life and of the problem of grown-ups. Too many adults forget, not that they *were* children, but *how* they were children! With many, the hurts and fears and dreams of those far-off days are buried too deeply to return vividly into consciousness. Happy are those who can understand children because they are able to remember emotionally their own childhood moods and ways.

Perhaps you recall a night-storm that threatened to destroy your trees? Momentary illumination by the jagged lightning revealed them struggling against the beating wind. But as the thunder subsided, you slept, and in the morning looked out upon the ground cluttered with broken branches, but the trees were standing, proudly victorious, erect and stately as ever! Perhaps they are still there—the trees of home! They survived that storm, and many others, because their roots were deeply embedded in the earth.

Beside Still Waters

Whatever else the years have taught, you have learned that storms are the inevitable experience of life. Rootage in the Eternal Verities enables triumph over tension and tragedy. You, like your childhood tree-friends, can remain serenely erect, holding your head high even though buffeted and bruised! When life's winter hurls its cold and snow, you, too, can remain patient and undismayed, knowing the certainty of spring! Deep within your being, as within the life centers of the trees, is peace and its assurance of renewed joys!

Across the years they smile; receive their kindly benediction—the trees of home!

18

On Joyful Wings

Exuberance and buoyancy characterize the gulls in their flight, as on strong wings they whirl and wheel with grace and beauty, skimming over the thundering surf. Joyfully they escort the sea-going ship, a feathered legion, their sentinels high in the rigging, watching eagerly for the galley's refuse—their daily banquet. Patrolling the beach-sands, and, at times, inland far from their native haunts, they snatch up edible debris. Scavengers they are; not friendly, yet friends of man.

On joyful wings they exemplify beauty. There is poetry in their flight, a rhythm of exertion and quiescence as they soar above the rolling sea and on motionless wings descend to ride the waves or balance themselves on tossing debris. Flight is accomplished by an alternation of effort and relaxation; climbing and then on rigid pinions, gliding to their destination.

"Behold the fowls of the air. . ."[1] admonished the Master. As with birds, so with us: the secret of joyous achievement is rest between successive efforts. Life, as music, has its rhythm of silence and

77

sound, of surging energy and quiet calm. The heart demonstrates it, following each beat with a period of repose. The activity-rest cycle is part of the rhythmic behavior of the human organism.

The Otherness in Whom "we live and move and have our being,"[2] Eternal Spirit, Infinite Wisdom, Divine Love, God—whatever term you may use to affirm this Reality—surrounds our lives no less than the air encompasses the gulls in their flight. When we grow quiet in the act of deliberate, articulate prayer or in the art of resting the mind in silent trust, which is prayer nonetheless, we are able to gain new strength. Prayer is not merely words directed to the Deity, be it whispered or shouted, eloquent or incoherent; more truly is it the act of relaxation that quietly opens the inner self to the inflow of the Divine Spirit.

In the attainment of serenity, there is no more rewarding self-discipline than relaxation as a part of the rhythm of life. When tension subsides, the mind clears, ability to think logically and creatively is engendered, decisiveness and strength are rejuvenated, vision comes into focus, and one looks upon the contemporary scene, or his own kaleidoscopic environment, with renewed composure and the assurance that there is a Purpose in life. The sense of a greater than human Presence begets confidence in the Eternal Balance of things. God is *All*, the ever-present Reality, "our refuge and strength"!

Life is more than feverish struggle: it is also quietness and confidence. In the duality of action and silence, effort and repose, life is kept fresh and vital, throbbing with energy, vibrant with harmony, and welling up from within, an unfailing fountain of creative joy! Set into tingling action are all the forces of the being, enabling us to meet life with adventurous expectancy. God would have us face each new day with thrilling eagerness, as on joyful wings!

Beside Still Waters

WINGS AGAINST THE WIND

Against the heavy head-winds I would rise,
Borne up by its force, yet with something of
    my own power
Bearing me closer to the turquoise skies
Through wide and windy spaces, hour by hour.
The wings of my spirit strong against the might
That would deter me upon my upward way,
Above me the racing clouds, below, the white
Drift of the sea, its silver spray.

I would have gulls' wings on my heavenly climb,
I would be stronger than the winds that blow,
I would lift up beyond all space and time —
There is a haven for me — I would go
With wings against the wind, with wings wide-
    spread.
There is splendor above me, there is light ahead!

Grace Noll Crowell [3]

19

River Reborn

Among your nature friends, is there a river born on glacial heights and, in its downward journey, wandering through a mountain valley? When the stream was shallow, rocks on its bed rose above the surface, causing nervous waters to fret into restless riffles; pools formed along its course and, with neither inlet nor outlet, became stagnant, ugly to see and to smell.

But the river was reborn! When the sun's heat sent waters cascading from high places, or, when storm-clouds burst, the river rose to fill, if not overflow, its banks. Then the stagnant pools were swept clean—absorbed in the fresh torrent. Obstinate rocks were submerged and forgotten. A surge of happy, singing waters moved in serene sureness, eager to spend themselves in joyous refreshment to thirsty lands beyond!

Human personalities, ofttimes, become stagnant when insulated; energy cannot get in because it cannot get out. Like the river, they need a new inflow of resources from beyond themselves, and a new outlet that creativity may flow through them.

To lose oneself in a worthy and challenging interest, is to find emotional stability, joyous contentment, creative influence. The abandonment of self to something greater than self transforms life— it becomes rich, sparkling, tingling with significance! One is swept out of himself; liberated from the irritating annoyances of shallow concerns, the fret of surface interests!

Find a cause for which to live—a purpose for which to give! Through the lavish outpouring of thought, enthusiasm, and abilities is realized the unfathomable joy of living deeply—serenely, creatively, triumphantly!

As with a river, so with a person: beauty, vibrancy and joy come with the abandonment of self, the out-flow of energies in unmeasured giving. God's gift to the giver is a new meaning and value to life —eagerness, hope, iridescence.

Thus, one becomes a creative force in an arid world. His: the ineffable joy of a true self-expression, abiding satisfaction, and the life that is life indeed—that which Jesus termed "life eternal," for it is life superlative!

Beside Still Waters

AS TORRENTS IN SUMMER

As torrents in summer
Half dried in their channels,
Suddenly rise, though the
Sky is still cloudless,
For rain has been falling
Far off at their fountains;

So hearts that are fainting
Grow full to o'erflowing,
And they that behold it
Marvel and know not
That God at their fountains
Far off has been raining!

Henry Wadsworth Longfellow [1]

20

Wingéd Rainbow

Among nature's creatures none is more enchanting in its loveliness or dramatic in its life cycle than the butterfly. More than 50,000 species of the Lepidoptera, in fabulous wing color and pattern, contribute to the beauty of our world. Covered with microscopic scales, their pigmented wings become iridescent through the refraction of sunlight.

On wings of rainbow hues, this dainty creature flutters between islands of fragrance: lovely blossoms stored with sustaining nectar. Having won their wings, life becomes an excursion of joy as they engage in their task of floral pollination. Sensitive beyond our imagination are the creatures' antennae, attuned to variegated fragrance; their enjoyment of odors nears intoxication.

Its dramatic metamorphosis marks the butterfly as the Cinderella of the insect world. This exquisite child of the air, before its reincarnation, was a lowly worm, often evil-smelling; and crawling, in

85

near blindness, to subsistence on bits of leaf and decaying vegetation. It was reborn from ugliness to beauty, not only in form and color but in the possession of a delicate fragrance.

Its saga is familiar. Emerging from the egg, it completed its larva stage and then created for itself a tomb; there in the darkness it lay. But within its disintegrating body resided the life-germ of a different kind of organism, destined to the adventure of life in a new environment. With infinite patience and arduous toil, the insect forced an opening in the wall of its cocoon and laboriously emerged, its wings damp and crumpled. Persistent exercise developed these until the new-born creature could embark upon its ecstatic career, drifting from blossom to blossom on luminous sails of joy.

Think not of the butterfly as fragile and ephemeral. True, some live briefly, but others for several years. With tremendous flying capacity they rival the birds in migration. Huge flocks of butterflies move *en masse* over continents and even oceans!

In this miracle of nature is a parable. Consider the transformation of insect appetite for bitter, inorganic matter to the purity of floral nectar! If one of God's lowly creatures can so change, may not man, His masterpiece, also be reborn to new appreciations and desires?

Think of the butterfly's rigorous toil in emerging from the chrysalis. . .what if it had yielded to inertia! As it used its rudimentary energy, new power was generated until, on wings of rainbow loveliness, it rose to the fulfillment of its mission of beauty and joy in God's creation. You, too, were born with wing capacity—wings for your spirit! To realize this potential, you also must strive. Spiritual strength does not come as an instantaneous gift; only by activating what you have, can you have more. Pray not for an increase of faith; you have enough to begin your upward career. Use what you have and you will possess more—all that you need! Faith and, indeed, all virtues are accumulative!

In the Wingéd Rainbow is an epitome of life itself and of its fullness! Beauty and joy are your destiny, too! Sing with the poet:

THE BUTTERFLY

I hold you at last in my hand,
   Exquisite child of the air;
Can I ever understand
   How you grew to be so fair?

From that creeping thing in the dust
   To this shining bliss in the blue!
God, give me courage to trust
   I can break my chrysalis, too!

Alice Freeman Palmer [1]

21

The Song Of Little Rivers

"Music belongs to all matter," said John Muir, "there is not a silent, songless particle in the Lord's creation." Much of this music we do not hear because its vibrations are outside the octaves of our perception; yet, there are in nature undertones and overtones of enchanting loveliness lost to us because in our noisy haste we do not pause to listen, to feel, to understand.

Water in motion is always vocal. Its loveliest voice is that of the meandering brook, as with soft and gentle tones it drips over rocks, glides across beds of sand, nuzzles its flower-embroidered banks. When thick branches of friendly trees shade it from the sun's heat, it responds with murmurs of contentment. Unexpected obstacles it greets with riffles of tinkling laughter.

As evening shadows fall, the gurgle of little rivers becomes more distinct, their peaceful cadences inducing a lovely sense of quiescence. In a loud and perplexing world, a quietly wandering stream epitomizes serenity. It is oblivious to man's haste and to the irritations that make his tranquility fragmentary.

Has life for you grown weary or sad? Turn from its irritations and tensions and listen again to singing waters. Recall the music of a friendly brook; recapture the charm of its melody; let its modulated tones quiet your spirit. Sense its calmness as beneath smiling skies it roams through green pastures and beside silent hills. Keep your heart attuned to its cadences of peace. Let nature's calmness banish confusion and care. You will receive the benediction of serenity bestowed upon those who can be still: to listen, to feel, to understand. And thus to know the reality of that which Tennyson avers, "There is no joy but calm."

THERE IS SWEET MUSIC HERE

There is sweet music here that
    softer falls
Than petals from blown roses
    on the grass,
Or night-dews on still waters
    between walls
Of shadowy granite, in a
    gleaming pass;
Music that gentlier on the
    spirit lies,
Than tired eyelids upon tired
    eyes;
Music that brings sweet sleep
    down from the blissful skies.
Here are cool mosses deep,
And thro' the moss the ivies
    creep,
And in the stream the long-
    leaved flowers weep
And from the craggy ledge the
    poppy hangs in sleep.

Beside Still Waters

Why are we weigh'd upon with
   heaviness,
And utterly consumed with
   sharp distress,
While all things else have rest
   from weariness?
All things have rest: why should we
   toil alone. . .
Nor steep our brows in slum-
   ber's holy balm;
Nor harken what the inner
   spirit sings,
"There is no joy but calm!"

Alfred Tennyson[1]

WIND IN THE PINE

Oh, I can hear you, God, above the cry
  Of the tossing trees—
Rolling your windy tides across the sky,
  And splashing your silver seas
    Over the pine,
   To the water-line
    Of the moon.
  Oh, I can hear you, God,
Above the wail of the lonely loon—
When the pine-tops pitch and nod—
   Chanting your melodies
Of ghostly waterfalls and avalanches,
Washing your wind among the branches
  To make them pure and white.

Wash over me, God, with your piney breeze,
  And your moon's wet-silver pool;
Wash over me, God, with your wind and night,
   And leave me clean and cool.

Lew Sarett[2]

22

Glowing Embers

How relaxing the warmth of burning logs as one lies under the open sky, its canopy of stars inducing tranquility and wonder! As flames die to glowing embers, the sky's lamps shine in splendor such as one never beholds from city streets. Forgotten are the paltry issues of the world—its man-made problems that vex and baffle, as eyes and minds are lifted to the panorama of God's hosts marching to their destiny in the cosmos' vast parade.

Remembered is the question of the Psalmist on that star-studded night of the long-ago: "When I consider Thy heavens, the work of Thy fingers, the moon and the stars which Thou hast ordained: what is man that Thou art mindful of him?" Came the answer: "Thou hast made him a little lower than the angels, and hast crowned him with glory and honor!"[1] *You* are His creation! You have a destiny in His purpose! You have a high estate: "a little lower than the angels!" Such assurance redeems from mediocrity and gives dignity to the soul.

Before the glowing embers, your heart is attuned to the serenity of the spangled heavens and the night-draped earth. You are quieted by the soft music of stirring boughs, lake-waters gently lapping the shore, the plaintive call of a distant loon. Then comes relaxation and serenity. God is near.

At dawn you will awaken to the music of a bird chorus. . .breathe deeply the light and zestful air. . .tingle to the invigorating shock of cold water dashed upon your face, or perhaps by a quick plunge into the lake itself. . .inhale eagerly the pungent odor of burning wood, as the campfire is renewed. . .rejoice in the day's promise of high adventure in God's out-of-doors.

Within glowing embers are caves of mystery: luminous corridors that open into memories and inspire dreams. Watching embers is not unlike following summer clouds; both are constantly changing, forming imaginative pictures. Let the embers' glow illuminate those mysterious corners of your mind where are lodged near-forgotten days. Bring forth memories to inspire and to bless!

Embers are also the material out of which dreams are made. Let your heart create visions filled with love and peace, pictures of what you can be and do. Such reveries are the creators of destiny! With rare insight, declared the Biblical writer: "For as he thinketh in his heart (as he dreams) so is he." Your potential is the self of your finest dreams, for you were made "a little lower than the angels"!

WOOD-FIRE

Now burns the fire with steadier radiance,
For now the flames no longer dance light-footed
Upon the wood, but, deeply penetrating,
Upon its dead heart feed their living glory
And turn its blackness into molten gold.

An inner glow matching the outer shining
Fills and o'erflows the silent worshipper. . .
If stolid wood can kindle to such flame,
If this rude cabin can be so transfigured
Into a temple fit for the abode
Of the blest spirits from the heavenly places,
What miracles of beauty, love, and joy
May yet be wrought from the full stuff of life?[2]

23

Triumph At Sunset

Clouds assume a leading role in the sunset drama. Always there is loveliness, even when no thunderheads impede the orb's declining course; yet, it is the sullen overcast, the struggle of sun against massed darkness that creates the setting for a gorgeous display of lambent color—emanations of light playing upon the lowering elements. The sun, rejoicing in his victory over storm-forces, spills joy in molten streams of breath-taking beauty, transforming the broken and scattering clouds into a flood of crimson splendor, bathing sky and earth with radiance!

Has your joy been overcast? Have pain, disappointment, loss, fear threatened your peace? Touched by the light of the Infinite, illuminated by Divine Love, your spirit may glow with triumph despite opposition, difficulty, even tragedy!

The Apostle speaks of those who in the soul's conflict are "more than conquerors."[1] In their victory is an over-plus of beauty, a radiance of spirit diffusing loveliness of courage and faith, a dramatic surge of lustrous grace. Let such triumph color your life, and those who see and feel will renew their faith. Let your influence be more than merely good: let it be beautiful, attractive, radiantly creative!

As you feel the stabbing splendor of the autumn sunset, its ecstatic brilliance enhanced by the struggle against threatening clouds, remember the words of the Psalmist—always a fitting prayer at sundown—"And let the beauty of the Lord, our God, be upon us"![2]

RIFT IN THE CLOUDS

When, under dripping skies, the day
has been dreary, how welcome a rift in
the clouds, how lovely the sun's smile!
His golden rays betoken victory: storm
forces are spent, lightning fades to
distant and infrequent illumination of
retreating clouds; thunder reverberates
from the far horizon, rolling as a weary
giant's guttural voice.

Tomorrow smiling skies will
bless the freshly washed earth!

Always the drama of contending forces
in nature ends with the victory of light:
creative warmth, renewed tranquility.

Ever the majestic sun
triumphs over storm and darkness.

Life, too, has its storms, when the spirit
is leaden under loneliness or pain, when
tragedy like falling lightning shatters joy.
Always God's forces struggle for the
renewal of faith with victory over despair.
Life's "shadows are all alive with light."

Beside Still Waters

Light shall break through the
gloom and bless the soul with peace!

Let the warm joy of the victorious sun
bathe your heart in its healing glow!
You are destined for triumph, not defeat;
for confidence, not fear; for joy, not
sorrow; live in anticipation of such
fulfillment. There is no finality in
clouds—they always disappear! The
unchanging, abiding reality in God's
world is light.

Look for the rift in your clouds!

THIS GOLDEN HOUR

An afternoon of rain, and now
   this saffron light!
With effulgence of gold on flower
   and leaf;
   The hour is sharp and clear
a time that's bright
   with beauty far beyond belief
And not a rain-drenched blade of
   grass
   or limestone rock,
is missed — but splendor-kissed,
While high above, the weathercock
   stands tethered in a golden tryst.

Mary Holman Grimes[3]

24

God's Love Is Falling With The Rain

On nature's symphony one of the loveliest strains is in the music of falling rain.

Let memory summon back to consciousness some of the feeling-tones in the sound of rain: an evening sprinkle, scarcely audible, whispering to lilac blooms, bidding them breathe forth more exquisite aroma. . .the tapping of a summer shower against window-panes where petulant child faces are pressed, impatient for fair skies and outdoor pleasures. . .staccato notes upon shingles above an old attic—childhood playground on a wet day, a realm of mysteries with heaped storage and the musty odor of ancient trunks. . .the pelting of huge drops upon a dry field and the quick smell of moistened dust . . .a quiet shower murmuring its benediction upon lawn and garden, with their response of mystical fragrance. . .the noisy deluge upon city streets channeled into a torrent dashing in quest of freedom. . .a cloud, with liquid laughter, pouring its contents upon a lake: water joining water in renewed camaraderie, for no drop is lost in nature's economy, water journeys between earth and sky in a never-ending cycle of blessing. . .and, perhaps, the dearest of all is the music of night rain upon the roof of cabin or tent: incomparable lullaby, invitation to tranquility and to refreshing sleep!

Rain nourishes and cleanses, becalms and awakens, renews and beautifies! Grass and soil, flowers and leaves respond with eagerness to its caress, and join in a song of gratitude to the Giver of all good. To our hearts its music brings contentment and serenity. Truly, God's love is falling with the rain!

RAIN ON THE ROOF

Rain on the roof;
    The sweet-voiced memory
    That rings across the years
    In silver melody.

Rain on the roof;
    A cottage weathered gray
    That knew the white gulls' cry,
    The tang of spindrift spray.

Rain on the roof;
    The garret's narrow stair,
    The snowy beds beneath
    The hand-hewn rafters there.

Rain on the roof;
    Against the fog-horn's wail,
    Grim banshee of the sea
    Who warns the periled sail.

Rain on the roof;
    Its drowsy rhythm kept,
    A pearl-lined lullaby,
    While little children slept.

Eleanor M. Tyler[1]

Beside Still Waters

LOVE IS FALLING IN THE RAIN

I think the sap of every spray
Leaps to a hidden tune today,
Bursting in music green and gay;
For love is falling in the rain,
Drenching the world to life again,
Splashing through the springtime air
Resurrection everywhere.

O, magic of the humble shower!
Cup-bearer to the smallest flower!
Stooping to pour the gift divine
In living streams of dewy wine
Where honey-suckles leap and twine!
Holding the cup to thirsty leaves
Of hawthorn bush and dogwood trees,
While little birds in every lane
Sing, "Love is falling in the rain"!

O, Mystery, to bend so low
That in a raindrop You might go!
O, Love, so intimate and small,
The breath, the bloom, the gift of all!
The Very Heart of every heart,
The end, the middle, and the start,
Above, below, within, without
O springtime blossoms, laugh and shout!
And soul, sing forth a high refrain,
Lifting a mad and happy strain,
For Love is falling in the rain!

Margaret Prescott Montague [2]

25

Blankets Of Peace

*F*og—sometimes a translucent veil, thinly golden in the October sun, flung about the shoulders of a hill; again, a dense cloud blanketing the valley; mellowing sound to a tone of unreality: the far-away call of a crow cutting thick silence. . .the sharp crunch of feet upon gravel. . .voices strange in the distance—muffled cadences emerging from the mist and drifting again to silence. . .and there is no stillness like the acute calm of concealing fog.

Whimsical is the fog: playing in and out of sheltered nooks, wrapping itself around high places, obscuring distances; yet, over the hill or around the bend, the air may be bright, the sky smiling; as of the wind, so of fog—one never knows "whence it cometh and whither it goeth."

Fascinating is mist-shrouded landscape: familiar lanes mysteriously different, ordinary structures distorted, old landmarks strangely new, prosaic woods an enchanted forest.

Assurance of Eternal Truth is in the clinging fog: reminder that beyond obstructed vision are well-known and loved realities. If you are bewildered, troubled, less sure of life's verities, feel anew the certainty that such values can be but momentarily dimmed. Although not seen, they are no less real; indeed, they may be more real! And ever beyond, clear skies smile!

Tranquility is engendered by the fog-eiderdown enfolding God's earth: cooling, softening, silencing, caressing, comforting.

Accept with grateful faith, God's blankets of peace!

MIST

The hills are dimmed to memories, in tiers
The town, a blue dream, turns to aging stone;
And all is blurred, as something seen through years,
That once was definite and near and known.
Like gladness time has reaped, the soft mist holds
The gold and scarlet of each separate tree—
A frozen mountain lost among its folds,
A river widening slowly to the sea.

The mist is passionless—it cools and stills
The fevers that are borne for beauty's sake;
With autumn flaming on a hundred hills,
It stills the heart that otherwise must break. . .
The mist that keeps the shaken soul secure
From more of rapture than it can endure.

Ada Hastings Hedges [1]

Beside Still Waters

MIST IN THE MOUNTAINS

Dawn mist makes a Chinese print
  Of this veiled scene,
The banks of pennyroyal and
    mint
  A wraith of green
Beside the colorless creek, the
     blue
  Of sky and the mauve
Of mountains blurred to a neutral
    hue,
The sprawling grove
Of aspens blotted out, and now—
  Sharp, dark,
Dripping jewels—one near bough
  Is a stark
Pen-scratch on the pale gouache
  Where all design
Is blurred, lost in a luminous
    wash,
Save this single artfully angled
    line.

Ethel Jacobson [2]

26

Fading Summer

ranquility broods over the landscape. Against the hills is flung a mystic veil of translucent haze. It is hot, as only September can be; yet a different kind of heat—in it is the prophecy of frost. Not yet has it come, even to the high places. Nature is holding her breath —the hot breath of fading summer. Not a stir of wind ripples the poplars to make their dry leaves querulous.

The air is charged with expectancy; every placid stream reflects it. Soon frost will come and waiting trees don garments of splendor; now they are poised on tiptoe, anticipating nature's cool kiss. Here and there, high on the hillside, some impatient bushes have assumed their brilliant garb—little spots of yellow amid the massed greenery.

The light is mellow with late summer, a summer that has lingered beyond her time and whose parching heat has colored the fields to russet, the hills to gray-brown. All nature is prepared to welcome the turn of the season—autumn with its sparkling dawns, and winter's first tentative smile. Soon it will come, with glistening snow on far mountain peaks and rain washing the valleys. A new zest will temper the air, quickening the step and ending this last lazy dream of summer. Fields and forests with bated breath await the first far-flung signal of impending change. Summer has had her languid day; she has overstayed; how welcome will be golden-garbed autumn!

God of the ever-changing seasons, recreating the earth in beauty, will temper your spirit: renewing, redeeming from monotony, cleansing and inspiring! Yield to His wisdom; let life's inevitable changes reveal new loveliness, as your heart beats in serenity, welcoming each new phase of nature's course. How swiftly the seasons pass! Do not resist time; rejoice in it as one of God's ministering angels! Receive His gift; the beauty and joy of life's autumn!

27

Majestic Individuality

How many leaves on a large maple tree? How many in a forest, in all the forests of the world? As winter's snowflakes, are they beyond counting? A scientist has estimated that in a normal snowstorm a million million flakes fall on one acre of ground. Probably even more numerous are the planets in space. Leaves, snowflakes and planets are beyond man's computation!

The wonder is not merely the countlessness in nature, but so infinitely varied are its units that no one has ever discovered two identical leaves or two identical snowflakes! It may be presumed that the same would be true of planets. It certainly is true of human entities. Individuality is one of creation's miracles. The infinite individuality of snowflakes, leaves, planets and human beings testifies to God's purpose for each unit.

Every leaf exists as an entity—separate, different, distinguishable from all others. Examine the leaf and marvel at its construction and function. It is a laboratory with complicated chemical processes: the green chlorophyll absorbs energy from the sun's rays, creates starch and converts it to sugars essential for the sustenance of the tree. Each

111

leaf is also an air-cooler, absorbing carbon dioxide from the atmosphere and releasing it in refreshing moisture—a delight to all who seek the tree's shade. After the season's service, flamboyantly colored in breath-taking beauty, the leaves drift to the ground, there to become part of another chemical process in nature's economy.

Uncountable billions of leaves, yet the mass functions as individuals, each with its own oneness! Here is a parable for human experience.

Whatever society may be or become, it is first of all individuals, no two exactly alike. This uniqueness gives to each person dignity and importance. There is only one *you!* When you entered this world, something different and distinctive came into being! Among the billions who have lived, are now living, or ever will live—there never has been and never will be another individual your exact counterpart! You are a special creation. And you attain significance because of what you yourself are, not because of what you possess or what your environment may momentarily be.

Why did God create *you?* Why do you, an entity possessing self-consciousness, exist? Your very uniqueness asserts that for your life there is purpose. If in creation, with its system of majestic individuality, "nothing walks with aimless feet," God has a plan for you. The environment in which you now find yourself may be yours by chance—call it coincidence or fate, as you will—nevertheless, none other could afford you greater opportunity for superlative living. Not your environment, but what you make of it, what you do with it, determines your life quality!

You are of consequence to God, as is all individuality in His creation. Jesus symbolically affirmed this truth: "Are not two sparrows

sold for a penny? And not one of them shall fall on the ground without your Father: but the very hairs of your head are all numbered."[1]
You are necessary to God: or you, an offspring of Divine Consciousness, would not now be reading these lines. To express God's purpose—that part of His infinite process involved in your unique individuality—gives you significance. Accept it with humility and reverence; let it also inspire serenity of spirit and abiding joy!

BENEATH THE WINTER STARS

How white the stars are in this inky blackness!
How strangely still the hills and hollows lie!
How cold beneath the passionless white fires
That burn like molten silver in the sky!
I am so small beneath their countless numbers,
So little and so lost in this vast dark,
I reach my hands to find some warmth and comfort
In fires a million light years off, each spark
Left smoldering from the white heat of creation:
Strange icy flames that have the power to sear
Upon my heart how truly unimportant
Is this small earth, and man's brief sojourn here . . .
And yet, and yet—recalling God's great mercy
In sending Christ to tread this planet's sod,
I straighten in the starlight, I grow taller,
Remembering my significance to God.

Grace Noll Crowell [2]

28

Autumn Mosaic

A riot of color—exciting, exhilarating,
sets hills and valleys aflame, and fills
the atmosphere with luminous beauty.

Autumn evokes a mood of elation: the crisp
air, fragrant with harvest tang, inspires a
spring to the step, a lilt to the spirit.

Well-being floods the senses.
The harvest is bountiful; orchard limbs bend
low with ripened fruit; nature's lush maturity
assures winter plenty.

The low voice of wind in the tree-tops, the
ecstatic song of a meadow-lark, the flamboyant
splendor of the hillside—incite one to sing
with Browning, "How fit to employ all the
heart and the soul and the senses forever
in joy!"[1]

Autumn is the season of moods and memories.
      Yield to its nostalgic influence:
shuffle through heaps of drifted leaves. . .
hear the music of their crisp rustle. . .
smell the sweet pungency of their burnings:
      nature's mystic incense. . .
rejoice in their gift to mother earth:
a thick carpet of variegated color. . .
feel the warmth of an October sun tempering
      the chill of impending frost.

And watch the leaves fall: a few
prematurely, as though impatient to
achieve fulfillment. . .others haltingly,
as though fearful of the brown mold—
their destiny. . .some, sodden with rain,
plummet dejectedly to the ground. . .a few
tragically cling beyond their time, sighing
in the chill wind—beaten, at last, from their
precarious hold by the storm's anger. . .yet,
most of the leaves fall serenely, even
flutter gaily, eager to take their places in
the Great Artist's autumn mosaic—their
vibrant colors shimmering in the radiant
sunlight, their brief flight as laughter
      beneath an azure sky.

Your life is a part of the Creator's human
mosaic: catch the serenity-tempo and joyous-
rhythm of His artistry; fulfill your destiny
as gallantly as do the leaves that make autumn
      golden and each tree a flame!

Beside Still Waters

Frosts must come; yes, but let them color your
spirit, that "the beauty of the Lord our God" may
be revealed in the triumph of your faith!

WINDS OF AUTUMN

Winds of Autumn, sharp and sweet,
Blow gold leaves about my feet;

Run swift fingers through my hair—
I shall laugh to find you there;

Run with light feet over grass,
Stirring fragrance as you pass;

Blow your music up the hollow,
Russet leaves will whirl and follow;

Winds of Autumn, blow my sorrow
Off into some far tomorrow!

Eleanor Allen[2]

29

Joyous Winter World

Earth's winter garment is multi-colored: from
brilliant white to soft pastels, varied with
delicate shades of purple, violet,
      blue and gray.

Forest snow cannot be sullied by city soot,
nor debased by traffic slush, nor polluted by
      urban debris.
Its purity and grace bless the forest family:
the fleecy blanket warms and comforts
      sleeping life.

The dazzling sun creates a fairyland, with
delicate shadow patterns of whitened branches.
And what beauty is more breath-taking than a
frosty moon smiling in benediction upon the
      quiet landscape!
The rushing stream, too busy for freezing,
greets with liquid chuckles the forest's
      arctic breath.

Let winter splendor stir your sense of wonder
before the handiwork of the Creator, Whose
every frost-flake is a lovely jewel of
      perfect symmetry.

Fresh snow in the forest: purity and serenity!
Would you possess its grace and peace?
Let the Infinite Artist recreate your
spirit and attune your mood to His
      joyous winter world!

30

Cabin In The Woods

Does the photograph of the log cabin in the woods provoke a nostalgic mood? If you have ever possessed such a hideaway, you know the excitement of returning to it from city or elsewhere. If yours has been only a dream cabin, that also has become a haven from life's tensions. Turning now from the complexities of modern living, in memory or in imagination, return to the simplicity of the primitive—to your cabin in the woods!

The snow muffles ordinary forest sounds and winter produces its own: the swish, as a laden branch drops its burden to the ground. . . the snap, as a frozen tree releases its tension. . .the crack, as an icicle breaks from the roof-edge and falls to soft berth in a cabin-side drift . . .the occasional flutter of wings, as a hopeful bird seeks sustenance.

Marked by forest traffic is the snow: deer passing cautiously to water; small life scurrying around the cabin, leaving erratic evidence of a frantic search.

121

After a tramp through the snow, warming to body and spirit is the hearth fire: cheery the dance of flames—they laugh with joy as they consume the pitch-filled wood, and the log's quick voice snaps its challenge to the retreating frost, which now congeals upon windows, forming a mosaic of fern patterns. Simple, the cabin chores: digging paths, carrying water, cutting wood.

How delightful the relaxation following healthy weariness from outdoor cold, and release from problems and pressures of ordinary life! Here in the stillness of the forest they recede in consciousness as you yield to the delicious languor of coming sleep, and deep within soft blankets dream of summer days with birds and blossoms, tree-filtered sunshine and the music of rain upon the cabin roof.

A brooding peace pervades the forest, the cozy cabin, and your own mind. You thank God for simple comforts and the elemental values of life. Tranquility floods your being.

New snow is falling, thick and heavy; all tracks will be lost in the covering whiteness. Tomorrow breath-taking beauty will be everywhere. The storm abating, brilliant sunshine will reveal myriads of jewels scattered throughout the forest, gracing every tree and bush.

Flames in the fireplace flicker as they pursue shadows across the walls and ceiling. Night's draperies fall noiselessly, as in God's protecting care you gratefully relax. Far away seem the world's turmoil and discord; gone are fevered frettings; your mind is filled with peace. You are renewed in spirit by a Divine healing. You will return to ordinary days and tasks refreshed, recreated, eager! Fulfilled is the promise of old, "In quietness and in confidence shall be your strength."

Come often to your cabin in the woods! Whether it be actual or only memory or imagination, it awaits to bless you with peace!

Beside Still Waters

DEER TRACKS IN SNOW

Like a shadow that remains
When the substance flees,
Lie the tracks you left behind
In new-fallen snow—and these
Imprints on the whitened ground
Speak your delicate fleet grace,
Softly sound your echo here
On this shadowed wintry space.

Alice Clear Matthews[1]

31

Winter Serenity

The season has changed. Nature's page has turned. The peace of autumn's Indian summer fades to the deep serenity of winter. Each season has its own distinctive emotional impact. Brood over this photograph of winter's first snow. Sense the serenity that spreads over valley and uplands. The beauty of the frosty country-side dispels fret and tumult and induces peace of mind.

The village has welcomed winter's first white gift. Yesterday the storm began with a fanfare of huge, moist flakes but soon settled into swirling clouds whipped by the wind from unsheltered roof-tops into deepening drifts as, hour by hour, earth's protecting blanket thickened. Before dawn the sky had emptied its first burden of snow, yet the sunrise was hidden by ominous banks of gray. The white backdrop of hills present an inky etching of trees in their bare auster-ity. It is a moody day.

Recorded on winter's clean page are the marks of morning adven-ture by wild life: footprints by muskrat, mink, and a timorous cot-tontail rabbit, tiny trails by field mice, disorder by raucous crows exploring a drift-sheltered corn shock. Smoke streams spiral lazily upward from village chimneys. Human activity begins to deface un-sullied snowfields; already plows are clearing roads, paths are being shoveled for traffic to school, store and mailboxes, the latter waiting in white-capped dignity upon their posts.

So begins the day. Its noises are vibrant in the frosty air: the distant sound of an axe against a stubborn log, the moan of a power-saw, the labored breath of motor vehicles, the shouts of children snowballing their way to school. Such is winter's inauguration, love-ly to see and hear and feel! It is more than mere weather with the sting of frost, it is a mood!

Village and farm homes are cozy with wood-fire warmth. Long evenings proffer leisure for books and hearth-side fellowship. Life's tempo is reduced. Nature's pulse beats more slowly.

Peace falls as softly as snow glides from laden branches of quiet trees; tranquility floods the mind: a gift from Divine Love—Winter Serenity!

Beside Still Waters

WINTER NIGHT

Come in and close the door.
Let the wind roar
outside; here we are snug.
The copper kettle's on, reflecting
        light
of curling flames against the bliz-
        zard night.
Sit near to me.
We'll stack some records for a
        symphony.
And see? —
we've flowers in the rug,
spring green among
them. What if the winter's old
and deeply cold?
Here in our house tonight
our love is bright
and warm with its own weather.
And we —
Oh, we are young
at any age, together!

Bonnie May Malody [1]

32

Voices Of The Winter Night

Winter's chill darkness broods over the quiet house.
The night's stillness is punctuated by common sounds
unnoticed during the day; now separated from the medley
of ordinary noises, they become distinctly
    voices of the winter night:

A train chugging breathlessly up the valley,
its whistle echoing from surrounding hills. . .
the metallic clatter of loose chains, as an automobile
struggles through growing drifts. . .the soft thud of
snow as a tree unloads its too-heavy burden. . .
the crash of an overgrown icicle hurtled from the roof
edge. . .a distant boom from the icebound lake—
homely sounds blending into the music of the winter
    wind, lyrical and lonely.

129

Nature's symphony has its wind instruments, also themes
peculiar to each season: the winds of spring are
hopeful, fresh and exhuberant. . .of summer, dry and
querulous. . .of autumn, brash and boastful, heavy
with harvest fragrance. . .but the winds of winter are
lonely and mournful, sighing for seasons gone, sobbing
for joys lost; breathing down chimneys, rushing around
house corners, ever whistling minor notes; busy piling
    the drifting snow.

Night sounds are muted by the soft blankets, as one
snuggles low with a sense of well-being and gratitude
for simple comforts. Voices of the winter night
induce relaxation and contentment. Serenity floods the
mind, for underneath are the Everlasting Arms:
Sustaining Energy, Unfailing Goodness, Divine Love,
    the Author of Life!

Beside Still Waters

SLEEP SWEETLY

Sleep sweetly in this quiet room
 O thou whoe'er thou art;
And let no mournful yesterday
 Disturb thy peaceful heart.

Nor let tomorrow mar thy rest
 With dreams of coming ill.
Thy Maker is thy changeless Friend,
 His love surrounds thee still.

Forget thyself and all the world,
 Put out each garish light;
The stars are shining overhead,
 Sleep sweetly then—good night![1]

33

As Winter Day Ends

The frigid day's vivid eventide suggests atonement by the sun for his inability to create warmth. Although he cannot bestow comfort, he will lavish beauty upon the valley, coloring its snow riffles with purple shadows, its open fields with variegated shades of violet, chestnut and steely blue. Rose-tinted skies soften to pink above the exquisite etching of forestry reaching to the far hills. There is a loneliness in the beauty of winter's early sundown, a sense of sadness as the light fades and shadows lengthen into growing darkness.

At times, the departing sun is attended by satellites—friendly escorts in his downward course: bright solar images, sometimes called "sun dogs" and regarded as the portent of dropping temperature. Early sunset seems to indicate an eagerness of the orb to escape the frigid hemisphere for milder climes. Boldly, the evening star appears, herald of an approaching host soon to bespangle the heavens.

As day fades toward the long and silent night, the cold intensifies. The Quaker poet described it:

A chill no coat, however stout,
Of homespun stuff could quite
    shut out,
A hard, dull bitterness of cold,
That checked, mid-vein, the
    circling race
Of life-blood in the sharpened
    face. [1]

A languor of weariness weighs down the body. Welcome is indoor comfort: relaxation before the penetrating cheer of blazing logs on the open hearth. Placidity is the physical reaction from combating the bitter elements. Drowsiness creeps on apace. Tranquility floods mind and spirit—a sense of well-being which is the prologue to deep and refreshing sleep.

Leave to God's protecting care tomorrow and its needs. "As thy days, so shall thy strength be"[2] is the divine assurance. Be not apprehensive of the future: if a crisis comes, you will know how to meet it. Tomorrow you will have strength for tomorrow! Need you ask more? "Divine Love always has met and always will meet every human need."[3]

Let your winter day end in serenity: in peace, the gift of God's love!

Beside Still Waters

THE SUNSET

Touched by a light that hath no name,
A glory never sung,
Aloft on sky and mountain wall
Are God's great pictures hung.
How changed the summits vast and old!
No longer granite-browed,
They melt in rosy mist; the rock
Is softer than the cloud;
The valley holds its breath; no leaf
Of all its elms is twirled:
The silence of eternity
Seems falling on the world.

John Greenleaf Whittier [4]

34

Again 'tis Spring!

Harbingers of spring are patches of old snow
settled amid trees, in the shelter of buildings,
or on shaded hill slopes: fading tokens of
winter's once mighty reign—reminders of days
when the landscape was blanketed with fresh
whiteness, and angry winds piled high the drifts.

Again, spring is releasing the winterbound earth!
Little rivulets flee joyously from softening
banks of gray snow; they sing of freedom, and
where they pause to form pools, their faces
reflect the smiling sky. Green shoots timidly
peer from the sun-warmed ground. Buds begin to
stretch. The wind sighs a fresh note of hope.
There is promise of renewal for all things.

As blurs of old snow—grim, wrinkled and worn—
glisten in the morning brightness, our spirits
share the lilt of a new song, a medley filled
with the tremulous hope of beauty yet to be.
Timid crocuses, bold pussywillows, smiling
trilliums—spring's pioneers—will soon
herald nature's miracle of renewed life.

Let the sparkling beauty of an early spring day
capture your mood. Further storms may come—
yet, they are but waning gasps of winter's icy
breath, for his reign is doomed. Life is
ascending! Nature will shortly renew the face
of the earth. Proclaimed by bird-fanfare, with
flower-pageant spring will come!

No less are God's restorative processes at
work in tired minds, pain-bound bodies,
troubled souls—releasing new tides of
health, stirring spirits to an upreach of
faith!

Share nature's recreative triumph! Let your
winter's gray weariness yield to the warm
beauty and vibrant joy of spring! Feel
now the eagerness and vitality of God's
renewing love. Lift up your heart and
sing!

For you—again 'tis spring!

Beside Still Waters

THE GOLDEN DAYS

O, golden are the days that we shall know,
  The dawns of purple and of magic made—
Nay, grieve not for the wistful Long Ago,
  And be not now afraid.
As children wiser grown, yet laughing still,
  Let us go hand in hand toward the blue;
As children standing on a morning hill—
  We shall be happy, too!

Look to the trees that dream their olden dream
  Of April come again to wake the bud,
Or hear the whisper of the patient stream
  That waits its joyous flood.
If your fond heart is sad a little while,
  This is but winter that will have its way—
Why, even now, along some country mile
  Falls the dear glance of May. . .

Ben Hur Lampman[1]

35

Spring Song

The winter-bound earth, released from inertia, awakens to new and joyous expressions.

Life is the theme of the spring song—a melody the intensity of which increases daily, nature's every cell vibrating to its rhythm. Joyous in music, rapturous in poetry is the theme of spring. It is a lyric of love and hope and growth. Ofttimes we are impatient; nature is slow in starting her springtime symphony; for weeks she seems to be tuning her instruments. Will spring ever come! we exclaim. Suddenly the Great Conductor lifts his baton—smiling skies, whispering winds, bursting buds, bird chirpings—all blend into the perfect melody! Deep within the earth, even through dark days, God has been at work, His unseen forces preparing for the glorious outburst—the renaissance of life!

Nor is it otherwise in human experience. When all is bleak and winterlocked, be sure that deeply within, divine forces are preparing for the miracle of new life. Your springtime is surely coming! Do winter moods now hold you? Are bodily functions inhibited? Are you afraid, perhaps without knowing why? Are you confused and unhappy, although for no articulate reason—darkened by an overhanging feeling of disharmony? Are you withdrawn from others as though frozen to inner rigidity?

Let winter yield to spring! Even as the inert and deadened earth beneath the warm sun pulses with new stirrings, let God's peace, the sense of well-being, of quickened energy flood your entire self! *Let spring come!* You cannot summon it any more than the barren garden can command growth, but you can turn toward God even as the earth on its axis turns toward the sun. And your receptivity will be blessed with restored joy. Your whole being will vibrate anew to the spring song—the symphony of life! Your equinox is at hand; let God awaken you to new and joyous expression! Let spring come!

PIPPA'S SONG

The year's at the spring,
The day's at the morn;
Morning's at seven:
The hillside's dew-pearled;
The lark's on the wing;
The snail's on the thorn;
God's in His heaven—
All's right with the world!

Robert Browning[1]

Beside Still Waters

NOW THAT SPRING IS HERE

Now that spring is here the old fields wear
Their beautiful new garments that are spun
From dew and moonlight, wind and rain
    and sun.
So shall I step from my dark frock of care
And put on gladness as the fields have done.

So shall I slip my cloak of weariness
From off my shoulders and be glad today,
New hope within my heart, and my new dress,
Threaded with faith and courage, shall be gay
As the shimmering flower-dotted fields today.

Grace Noll Crowell [2]

36

The Wind Passes By

No more enchanting music has nature
than that of wind playing upon the
   many-keyed organ of forestry.
Every needle, every leaf, every twig
contributes harmony: soft summer
undertones when lazy leaves stir. . .
rich winter crescendos as cedar and fir
bow before strong blasts. . .minor notes
in the groan of gnarled trunks and
limbs twisted by the savage tempest;—
music rises in cadences of power
and sinks to gentle whispers as
        the wind passes by.

Spring wind incites exhilaration with its
promise of renewal; earth's sleepers
begin to stir at its awakening touch;
buds, enfolded in their tiny casements,
        commence to stretch.
The wind hurries on its way, busy
with nature's errands—freshening,
invigorating, energizing the dormant earth.
Let it also cleanse your mind, sweeping
away hurts, frustrations, disappointments—
breathing into your heart the excitement
        of springtime renewal!

Watch how the trees greet the wind—not
resisting in stern rigidity, but bending
with it in cheerful indulgence, and after
it passes returning to normal posture:
rootage makes possible their elasticity.
So in human experience: tensions, stresses,
strains need not break the spirit, for
inner tranquility affords rootage; the
relaxed individual possesses resiliency
and sways with life's storms, yet always
        returns to erect composure.

Listen to the laughter of the trees playing
with the wind: they clap their hands, with
vibrant confidence they sing,
        gay and expectant.

Beside Still Waters

We humans need an antidote to brittle
rigidity—a sense of humor that prevents
taking ourselves too seriously; a buoyancy
that enables us to preserve an infectious
gaiety of spirit amid the tensions of daily
living, and poise despite the dizzy
    whirl of activities.

The badge of a tranquil spirit?
A quiet, joyous flexibility as
    "the wind is passing by"!

WHO HATH SEEN THE WIND?

Who hath seen the wind?
    Neither you nor I.
But when the trees bow down their heads,
    The wind is passing by.

Who hath seen God?
    Neither you nor I.
But when the men bow down their heads,
    Then God is passing by.

Glenn Clark[1]

37

When Evening Shadows Fall

Of all sunsets, those of spring are the most tender, the most poignant in their beauty.

When the sun has fulfilled his course and drops behind purple hills, a softening radiance, with exquisite loveliness, lingers over sky and land and water. In early twilight the birds dart and soar, busy with their home-building; as shadows lengthen, they rehearse their matins and then rest before their outburst of dawn melody. Spring winds croon their softest lullabies, caressing nature's babes now restless in their bud-cradles. Wherever frogs are assembled, with vibrant voices they join in the spring song. Masses of fleecy clouds radiate lingering pastels in the color symphony.

The waning day induces a pensive mood. In the sunset afterglow there is a wistful beauty, a tender quietness, as evening shadows fall. One feels the analogy in human experience.

149

Life, too, has its afterglow. Grateful we are for those who have shared with us earth's beauty, rejoiced in it, loved it and now, beyond the sunset, have entered upon the Adventure Splendid. Pioneers they are in new realms of beauty. Faith declares that the loveliest we mortals know are but hints of the ineffable grandeurs that await beyond: which "eye hath not seen, nor ear heard, neither have entered into the heart of man."[1] Those who have passed from our sight and touch have left in consciousness an afterglow: a lingering radiance, a haunting loveliness, an abiding blessing.

When evening shadows fall, may we leave in the consciousness of those whom we love, an endowment of tender beauty, a joy to be cherished, a lilting hope, a buoyant faith, and an afterglow of peace!

THE SUN, HIS COURSE FULFILLED

The sun, his course
   fulfilled,—
His glorious course, rejoicing earth
   and sky,—
In the soft evening, when the winds
   are stilled,
Sinks where his islands of refreshment lie,
And leaves the smile of his departure
   spread
O'er the warm-colored heaven and
   ruddy mountainhead.

William Cullen Bryant[2]

Beside Still Waters

A GOOD VISIT

Going, a good friend, a loved one,
does not take from the house warmth and
        light,
leaving rooms in the blight
of shadow. His presence is a sun
with a long afterglow. It lies on
the walls, coloring them
with beauty, like a precious gem
flowing, long after he is gone.

Helen Harrington[3]

BENEDICTION

Until the sunset's last soft glow
In benediction ends the day,
God's peace attend your onward path,
His love o'er shadow all your way.

Raymond B. Walker[4]

38

Blossoms Unlimited

The valley is vibrant with color—drifts of beauty, as spring a-wakens nature's lavish creativity. Across the land, thousands of orchards burst into splendor, with blossoms, not in paltry billions, but with a profusion utterly baffling to mathematics and even imagination! Every lovely bloom is eager to yield fruit; yet comparatively few will do so. A vast blossom excess testifies to nature's boundless provision: margins of safety against impoverishment.

The same prodigality characterizes the seed harvest—more than can possibly grow and produce, a surplus assuring preservation of the species. Lavishness is an obvious feature of nature. A Chinese proverb declares, "any fool can count the number of seeds in an apple, but nobody can count the apples in a seed"; the seed multiplies trees and apples and seeds beyond computation. Nature's redundance is a revelation of the Creator's wisdom in the perpetuity of His handiwork!

A similar divulgence lies in the infinity of energy: on this planet, the potential within the atom—oceans of dynamic power locked

153

within a handful of sand; and out on the fringes of observable space, in the mysterious and uncountable "quasi-stellar sources"—huge energy producing masses, each a hundred million times the size of our sun! What is the Creator's purpose in such immensities? What is the function of such power surplus in the cosmic pattern? The mind of man has no answer!

Physical resources are paralleled by reserves of mental and spiritual power. Tremendous achievements have been accomplished by tapping the hidden forces of personality, yet, potentiality is always far in advance of attainment; no one has ever fully expressed his capabilities.

"In quietness and in confidence shall be your strength"[1]—that is: gain such control over thought and feeling that you can dismiss inhibitions, relax the mind as well as the body, and experience an inflow of power adequate to the demands upon you. From the mysterious reservoir of energy below the threshold of consciousness, in time of emergency comes reinforcement of ordinary strength. Remember when you face extraordinary demands, that you possess extraordinary resources—an energy surplus adequate to exceptional needs. Tension and fear are inhibitors; serenity and faith are liberators of your reserves.

Available beyond your own powers are accesses of strength in the Eternal—"in Him we live, and move, and have our being."[2] Somewhere, somehow, energy from the Infinite vitalizes the finite. "My help cometh from the Lord which made heaven and earth."[3] They that wait upon the Lord shall renew their strength."[4] Such realization of God's ever-available abundance gives joyous implications to the affirmation, "I shall not want!"

Beside Still Waters

Why should you want when boundless resources are at hand? Rejoice in the Divine munificence! His mercy is everlasting, His goodness beyond understanding, His love unwearied and without limit!

Sense the miracle of creation in the orchard's superabundance of blossoms. A utilitarian surplus? Yes, but more—a bonus of beauty! Ours is a world extravagant with color: amber dawns, flaming sunsets, variegated shades and tints spread over hills and valleys, radiations which bathe the soul in wonder and peace! God has made our world infinitely lovely! It vibrates with joy!

Obviously, God's will for all His children is an abundant life; health of body, emotional equilibrium, intellectual growth, spiritual maturity marked by confidence and courage, iridescent personality aglow with qualities that attract and inspire. Such is His will for you —not mere existence, but life abundant: rich, full, and eternal!

That which is possible for you to be and do, you can be and do! "All things are possible to him that believeth," declared the Master.[5] Let your self-image be worthy of Divine Love and Purpose!

> If our love were but more simple,
> We should take Him at His word;
> And our lives would be all sunshine
> In the sweetness of our Lord![6]

39

Forever Comes The Dawn

The day, golden and amber-tinted, glides through the draperies of dawn. Sunsets are more familiar but not more beautiful or dramatic. And when is daybreak more glorious than in the spring? Indeed, spring, the vernal equinox, is nature's own dawn.

In the day's youth, as always in youth, life is enchanting—its loveliness and mysticism more poignantly felt, the lure of the unknown more compelling. The heart, quickened by dawn-freshness, sings that the day will bring some loveliness. With such a beginning, anything seems possible!

Salute the dawn with expectation! Meet it on tiptoe! Even though lurking in the hours ahead may be discomfort, gray tasks, and unlovely situations, early moments of prayer and thanksgiving will temper the spirit for aught that comes. To meet God "in the cool of the day" is to renew confidence and courage and strength.

Breathe deeply the fragrant night-kissed air; let the dawn breeze, light and zestful, fan your spirit; open your heart to the joy of the vibrant bird chorus. Attune your senses to the awakening world. Let

God's peace, warm and alive, flow through your being, inducing adequacy for whatever the day may bring.

Dawn is the eternal reality. Sunset is only the prologue to dawn and is God's promise that there will always be sunrise. The morrow will bring not only a new day but a new world: one you have never known before, a world filled with undreamed-of possibilities. It is God's gift to you—receive it in humility and with joy!

To the ancient watchman was hurled the weary question, "What of the night?"[1] Came his jubilant assurance, "The morning cometh!"[2] So shall it ever be through life's darkness "until the day break and the shadows flee away"![3] Keep your heart eager and expectant. After the winter, springtime; after the night-shadows, sunrise; after quietness and confidence, strength! God's smile is in the dawn, also His beckoning to Adventures unlimited!

Forever comes the dawn!

THE SALUTATION OF THE DAWN

Listen to the Exhortation of the Dawn!
    Look to this Day!
For it is Life, the very Life of Life.
In its brief course lie all the
Verities and Realities of your Existence;
    The Bliss of Growth,
    The Glory of Action,
    The Splendor of Beauty;
For Yesterday is but a Dream,
And Tomorrow is only a Vision;
    But Today well lived makes
Every Yesterday a Dream of Happiness,
And every Tomorrow a Vision of Hope.
Look well therefore to this Day!
Such is the Salutation of the Dawn. [4]

Acknowledgments And Sources

ACKNOWLEDGMENTS AND SOURCES

The Bible: all scriptural quotations used in this book are from the King James Version of *The Bible.*

Mrs. Walker desires to acknowledge her personal gratitude to the persons and publishers who have so graciously allowed the use of the quotations and poems Dr. Walker had selected for inclusion in *Beside Still Waters;* especially all those dear friends whose interest in Dr. Walker's writings gave encouragement to her in the time and effort of making this book a reality.

Introduction—The Quest for Serenity
1. Proverbs 23:7
2. Isaiah 30:15
3. "The Certain Calm," Ethel Romig Fuller in *White Peaks and Green*, Metropolitan Press, Portland, Oregon 1933.
4. "Mine," Peggy James, *Arizona Highways*, Phoenix, Arizona.

Chapter 1—Green Pastures
1. Psalms 23

Chapter 2—Rejoicing in Beauty
1. Genesis 1:31
2. From "Hymn to Joy" in *Poems of Henry Van Dyke* by permission of Charles Scribner's Sons, New York, N.Y.
3. Genesis 3:8
4. "This Is My Father's World," Maltbie D. Babcock from *Thoughts for Everyday Living*, by permission of Charles Scribner's Sons, New York, N.Y.
5. "For the Beauty of the Earth," Folliott S. Pierpoint, *The Pilgrim Hymnal*, The Pilgrim Press, Boston, Mass., 1945.

Chapter 3—To Love a Garden
1. "My Garden," Thomas Edward Brown, 1830-1897.

Chapter 4—Moment of Splendor
1. Psalms 19:1
2. From "The Kingdom of God," Francis Thompson, 1859-1907.
3. "The World," Richard Realf, 1834-1878.
4. "God Is at the Anvil," Lew Sarett from *Covenant with Earth: a Selection from the Poetry of Lew Sarett*, edited and copyrighted, 1956, by Alma Johnson Sarett. Gainsville: University of Florida Press, 1956. Reprinted by permission of Mrs. Sarett.

Chapter 6—Waters That Laugh and Sing
1. Matthew 17:20
2. Genesis 1:31
3. Zephaniah 3:17
4. From "The Brook," Alfred Tennyson, 1809-1892.

Beside Still Waters

Chapter 7—The Silences of God

1. Psalms 46:10
2. "I Have Known a Sound," Grace Noll Crowell from *Between Eternities*, copyright 1944 by Harper & Row, Publishers, New York, N.Y.; permission for use granted by Harper & Row, Publishers, Inc.

Chapter 8—Seaside Healing

1. Author unknown.

Chapter 9—God's Mirror

1. "Out in the Fields with God," Elizabeth Barrett Browning, 1806-1861.
2. "In a Quiet Valley," Grace Noll Crowell, from *Light of the Years*, copyright 1936 by Harper & Row, Publishers, Inc., of New York, N.Y.; permission for use granted by Harper & Row, Publishers, Inc.

Chapter 10—Our Daily Bread

1. From "Our Daily Bread," Maltbie D. Babcock.
2. From "The Coming of Twilight," Florence E. Glazier.
3. John 16:24
4. "Bread," Ethel Romig Fuller from *White Peaks and Green*, Metropolitan Press, Portland, Oregon 1933.

Chapter 11—Beyond the Horizon

1. From "Goin' Home," William Arms Fisher.

Chapter 12—Vistas of Peace

1. Psalms 121:1
2. John Muir, 1838-1918.
3. "Who Knows a Mountain?" Ethel Romig Fuller from *White Peaks and Green*, Metropolitan Press, Portland, Oregon, 1933.

Chapter 13—The House and the Road

1. Psalms 46:1
2. Psalms 121:8

Chapter 14—Ships of Rest

1. Proverbs 3:24
2. "The Words of God," Samuel Taylor Coleridge, 1772-1834.
3. "How Lovely Is the Hand of God," author unknown.

Chapter 17—The Trees of Home

1. Author unknown.

Beside Still Waters

Chapter 18—On Joyful Wings

1. Matthew 6:26
2. Acts 17:28
3. "Wings Against the Wind," Grace Noll Crowell, from *Facing the Stars,* copyright 1931 by Harper & Row, Publishers, New York, N.Y.; permission for use granted by Harper & Row, Publishers, Inc.

Chapter 19—River Reborn

1. "As Torrents in Summer," Henry Wadsworth Lonfellow, 1807-1882.

Chapter 20—Winged Rainbow

1. "The Butterfly," Alice Freeman Palmer, 1855-1902.

Chapter 21—The Song of Little Rivers

1. From "The Lotos-Eaters," Alfred Tennyson, 1809-1892.
2. "Wind in the Pine" from *Covenant With Earth: a Selection from the Poetry of Lew Sarett.* Edited and copyrighted, 1956, by Alma Johnson Sarett. Gainsville: University of Florida Press, 1956. Reprinted by permission of Mrs. Sarett.

Chapter 22—Glowing Embers

1. Psalms 8:3-5
2. Author unknown.

Chapter 23—Triumph at Sunset

1. Romans 8:37
2. Psalms 90:17
3. "This Golden Hour," Mary Holman Grimes. Reprinted by permission from *The Christian Science Monitor.* © 1967 The Christian Science Publishing Society. All rights reserved.

Chapter 24—God's Love Is Falling with the Rain

1. "Rain on the Roof," Eleanor M. Tyler from *Singing Firs,* 1945.
2. "Love Is Falling in the Rain," Margaret Prescott Montague. Quoted by permission of *The North American Review* and the University of Northern Iowa, Cedar Falls, Iowa.

Chapter 25—Blankets of Peace

1. "Mist," Ada Hastings Hedges, in *Northwest Verse,* The Caxton Printers, Ltd., Caldwell, Idaho, 1931.
2. "Mist in the Mountains," Ethel Jacobsen. Reprinted by permission from *The Christian Science Monitor.* © 1965, The Christian Science Publishing Society. All rights reserved.

Beside Still Waters

Chapter 27—Majestic Individuality
1. Matthew 10:29, 30
2. "Beneath the Winter Stars," Grace Noll Crowell, from *Facing the Stars*, copyright 1941 by Harper & Row, Publishers, New York, N.Y.; permission for use granted by Harper & Row, Publishers, Inc.

Chapter 28—Autumn Mosaic
1. Robert Browning, 1812-1889.
2. "Winds of Autumn," Eleanor Allen in *Northwest Verse*, The Caxton Printers, Ltd., Caldwell, Idaho, 1931.

Chapter 30—Cabin in the Woods
1. "Deer Tracks in the Snow," Alice Clear Matthews. Reprinted by permission from *The Christian Science Monitor.* © 1966 The Christian Science Publishing Society. All rights reserved.

Chapter 31—Winter Serenity
1. "Winter Night," Bonnie May Malody. Reprinted by permission from *The Christian Science Monitor.* © 1968 The Christian Science Publishing Society. All rights reserved.

Chapter 32—Voices of the Winter Night
1. "Sleep Sweetly," author unknown.

Chapter 33—As Winter Day Ends
1. From "Snow-Bound," John Greenleaf Whittier, 1807-1892.
2. Deuteronomy 33:25
3. Mary Baker Eddy in *Science and Health with Key to the Scriptures*, page 494, lines 10-11, published by The First Church of Christ, Scientist, in Boston, Massachusetts, and used with permission of The Christian Science Board of Directors.
4. "The Sunset," John Greenleaf Whittier, 1807-1892.

Chapter 34—Again 'Tis Spring
1. From "The Golden Days," Ben Hur Lampman, from *How Could I Be Forgetting?*, Binford & Mort, Publishers, Portland, Oregon 1956.

Chapter 35—Spring Song
1. "Pippa's Song," from *Pippa Passes* by Robert Browning, 1812-1889.
2. "Now That Spring Is Here," Grace Noll Crowell, from *Facing The Stars.* Copyright 1941 by Harper & Row, Publishers, New York, N.Y. Permission for use granted by Harper & Row, Publishers, Inc.

Chapter 36—The Wind Passes By
1. "Who Hath Seen The Wind?" Glenn Clark. Reprinted with permission of Macalester Park Publishing Company, St. Paul, Minnesota.

Beside Still Waters

Chapter 37—When Evening Shadows Fall

1. Corinthians 2:9
2. "The Sun, His Course Fulfilled," William Cullen Bryant, 1794-1878.
3. "A Good Visit," Helen Harrington. Reprinted by permission from *The Christian Science Monitor.*© 1961 The Christian Science Publishing Society. All rights reserved.
4. "Benediction," Raymond B. Walker, author of this book.

Chapter 38—Blossoms Unlimited

1. Isaiah 30:15
2. Acts 17:28
3. Psalms 121:2
4. Isaiah 40:3
5. Mark 9:23
6. "There's a Wideness in God's Mercy," Frederick W. Faber, from *The Pilgrim Hymnal*, The Pilgrim Press, Boston, Mass., 1935.

Chapter 39—Forever Comes the Dawn

1. Isaiah 21:11
2. Isaiah 21:12
3. Song of Solomon 2:17
4. "The Salutation of the Dawn" from the Sanskrit.